Instant Penetration Testing: Setting Up a Test Lab How-to

Set up your own penetration testing lab using practical and precise recipes

Vyacheslav Fadyushin

[PACKT] PUBLISHING

BIRMINGHAM - MUMBAI

Instant Penetration Testing: Setting Up a Test Lab How-to

Copyright © 2013 Packt Publishing

All rights reserved. No part of this book may be reproduced, stored in a retrieval system, or transmitted in any form or by any means, without the prior written permission of the publisher, except in the case of brief quotations embedded in critical articles or reviews.

Every effort has been made in the preparation of this book to ensure the accuracy of the information presented. However, the information contained in this book is sold without warranty, either express or implied. Neither the author, nor Packt Publishing, and its dealers and distributors will be held liable for any damages caused or alleged to be caused directly or indirectly by this book.

Packt Publishing has endeavored to provide trademark information about all of the companies and products mentioned in this book by the appropriate use of capitals. However, Packt Publishing cannot guarantee the accuracy of this information.

First published: March 2013

Production Reference: 1210213

Published by Packt Publishing Ltd.
Livery Place
35 Livery Street
Birmingham B3 2PB, UK.

ISBN 978-1-84969-412-4

www.packtpub.com

Credits

Author
Vyacheslav Fadyushin

Reviewers
Igor Minin
Oleg Minin

Acquisition Editor
Jonathan Titmus

Commissioning Editor
Priyanka Shah

Technical Editor
Lubna Shaikh

Project Coordinator
Sneha Modi

Proofreader
Maria Gould

Graphics
Aditi Gajjar

Production Coordinator
Conidon Miranda

Cover Work
Conidon Miranda

About the Author

Vyacheslav Fadyushin graduated from the Novosibirks State Technical University. He holds a Master's degree in Comprehensive Information Security of Automated Systems. He started as a lead information security officer at a power engineering company and continued as a lead information security consultant. Vyacheslav acquired a lot of diverse experience and skills while performing various information security audits, consulting, and penetration testing projects with major CIS companies. Being an experienced information security consultant and penetration tester, at present, he lives and works in Berlin and continues his professional activity, performing both management and methodological functions as well as security assessments.

Vyacheslav currently works for ImmobilienScout GmbH.

The following are a few of Vyacheslav's other publications:

- *Information Security Log Management System, III Russian theoretical and practical Information Security Problems Internet conference, 2008*
- *Overall Wi-Fi security, Information Security magazine* (www.infosec.ru), *2010*

About the Reviewers

Igor Minin is a full-time Professor in the Siberian State Geodesy Academy, Russia. He was the Chief Research Scientist at the Institute of Applied Physics, Novosibirsk, Russia, from 1982 to 2000. Dr. Minin received a BA in Physics from the Novosibirsk State University, a PhD in Physics from Leningrad Electro-Technical University in 1986, and a Doctor of science degree from NSTU in 2002. Dr. Minin has over twenty years of international industrial and academic experience, and has played key roles in a number of projects, including hidden data and transfer technology in THML files and antiterrorism applications.

He is the author or coauthor of approximately 350 research articles, seven monographers (including *Diffractive Optics of Millimeter Waves* (IOP Publisher, 2004), and *Basic Principles of Fresnel Antenna Arrays* (Springer, 2008), and has been awarded 24 patents and inventions. He is the author of several books and book chapters in technical publications. He has been the editor of several books, including *Microwave and Millimeter Wave Technologies, Modern UWB Antennas, and Equipment* (IN-TECH, 2010) and *Microwave and Millimeter Wave Technologies from Photonic Bandgap Devices to Antenna and Applications* (IN-TECH, 2010).

Dr. Minin's research interests are in the areas of millimeter-wave and THz photonics and nanophotonics, information security, hidden different data in HTML and secret digital sign as well as development of antiterrorism devices, calculation experiment technologies, and explosive physics.

He is a member of SPIE, COST-284, and COSTc0603. Prof. Minin has been an invited lecturer at several international universities and institutions, among them the IEEE Singapore EMCS Chapter, and has served on a number of national and international conference committees. For his work, Dr. Minin was awarded the Commendation for Excellence in Technical Communications (LaserFocus World, 2003), and commendation by the Minister of Defense of Russia, 2000. Dr. Minin was included in Marques Who's Who in Science and Engineering. He is a full-time professor at the Siberian State Geodesy Academy, Russia.

The following are a few books that he has worked on:

- *Diffractive Optics of Millimeter Waves* (IOP Publisher, 2004)
- *Basic Principles of Fresnel Antenna Arrays* (Springer, 2008)
- *Microwave and Millimeter Wave Technologies Modern UWB Antennas and Equipment* (IN-TECH, 2010)
- *Microwave and Millimeter Wave Technologies from Photonic Bandgap Devices to Antenna and Applications* (IN-TECH, 2010)
- *Computational Fluid Dynamics Technologies and Applications* (IN-TECH, 2011)
- *Microsensors* (IN-TECH, 2011)
- *Ultrasound Imaging* (IN-TECH, 2011)
- *Radiovision methods for terrorism struggle* (*in Russian*, NSTU, 2008)

Oleg Minin is a full-time Professor and the head of the metrology and certification division in the Siberian State Geodesy Academy, Russia. He was the Chief Research Scientist at the Institute of Applied Physics, Novosibirsk, Russia from 1982 to 2000. Dr. Minin received a BA degree in Physics from the Novosibirsk State University. A PhD in Physics from Tomsk State University in 1987, and a Doctor of Science from NSTU in 2002, Dr. Minin has over twenty years of international industrial and academic experience, and has played key roles in a number of projects, including three-dimensional millimeter-wave real-time imaging and antiterrorism applications.

He is the author or coauthor of approximately 350 research articles, seven monographs including *Diffractive Optics of Millimeter Waves (JOP Publisher, 2004)*, and *Basic Principles of Fresnel Antenna Arrays (Springer, 2008)*, and has been awarded 24 patents and inventions. He is the author of several books and book chapters in technical publications.

Dr. Minin's research interests are in the areas of diffractive optics and antenna experiments (including explosive plasma antennas), millimeter-wave and THz photonics and nanophotonics, inftormation security, detection of hidden weapons as well as development of antiterrorism devices, experiment technologies, explosive physics.

He is a member of SPIE, COST-284, and COST-ic0603. Prof. Minin has been an invited lecturer at several international universities and institutions, and has served on a number of national and international conference committees. For his work, Dr. Minin was awarded the Commendation for Excellence in Technical Communications (LaserFocus World, 2003) and a commendation by the Minister of Defense of Russia, 2000. Dr. Minin was included in Marques Who's Who in the World.

The following are a few books that he has worked on:

- *Diffractive Optics of Millimeter Waves (IOP Publisher, 2004)*
- *Basic Principles of Fresnel Antenna Arrays (Springer, 2008)*
- *Microwave and Millimeter Wave Technologies Modern UWB Antennas and Equipment (IN-TECH, 2010)*
- *Microwave and Millimeter Wave Technologies from Photonic Bandgap Devices to Antenna and Applications (IN-TECH, 2010)*
- *Computational Fluid Dynamics Technologies and Applications (IN-TECH, 2011)*
- *Microsensors (IN-TECH, 2011)*
- *Ultrasound Imaging (IN-TECH, 2011)*
- *Radiovision methods for terrorism struggle (in Russian, NSTU, 2008)*

www.PacktPub.com

Support files, eBooks, discount offers and more

You might want to visit `www.PacktPub.com` for support files and downloads related to your book.

Did you know that Packt offers eBook versions of every book published, with PDF and ePub files available? You can upgrade to the eBook version at `www.PacktPub.com` and as a print book customer, you are entitled to a discount on the eBook copy. Get in touch with us at service@packtpub.com for more details.

At `www.PacktPub.com`, you can also read a collection of free technical articles, sign up for a range of free newsletters and receive exclusive discounts and offers on Packt books and eBooks.

PACKTLIB®

`http://PacktLib.PacktPub.com`

Do you need instant solutions to your IT questions? PacktLib is Packt's online digital book library. Here, you can access, read and search across Packt's entire library of books.

Why Subscribe?

- Fully searchable across every book published by Packt
- Copy and paste, print and bookmark content
- On demand and accessible via web browser

Free Access for Packt account holders

If you have an account with Packt at `www.PacktPub.com`, you can use this to access PacktLib today and view nine entirely free books. Simply use your login credentials for immediate access.

Instant Updates on New Packt Books

Get notified! Find out when new books are published by following `@PacktEnterprise` on Twitter, or the Packt Enterprise Facebook page.

Table of Contents

Preface   **1**

Instant Penetration Testing: Setting Up a Test Lab How-to   **7**
   Understanding penetration testing (Must know)   7
   Planning the lab environment (Should know)   13
   Setting up the network security lab (Must know)   21
   Setting up a web app lab (Should know)   47
   Setting up a Wi-Fi lab (Become an expert)   69
   Reviewing online lab portals (Become an expert)   79

Preface

Instant Penetration Testing: Setting Up a Test Lab How-to is a practical guide, which will help you to complexly approach the lab building process and save your time for practicing and gathering useful skills. You will learn how to plan the lab architecture and how to implement it using cost-saving solutions in an easy way.

What this book covers

Understanding penetration testing (Must know) shows what is penetration testing and how it is usually done.

Planning the lab environment (Should know) shows how to plan your lab environment.

Setting up the network security lab (Must know) describes the necessary steps to set up a lab for practicing overall penetration testing.

Setting up the WebApp lab (Should know) describes the necessary steps to set up a lab for practicing web application penetration testing.

Setting up the Wi-Fi lab (Advanced) describes the necessary steps to set up a lab for practicing wi-fi penetration testing.

Reviewing online lab portals (Advanced) provides a quick review of the online penetration testing labs.

Preface

What you need for this book

The following is a list of the software required:

- Virtualization software:
    - VMware Workstation 8
- Windows Servers:
    - Microsoft Windows Server 2008
    - Microsoft Windows Server 2003
- Windows Workstations:
    - Microsoft Windows XP
    - Microsoft Windows 7
- Linux server:
    - Ubuntu Server 12.04LTS
- Miscellaneous tools:
    - XAMMP for Windows
    - Mozilla Firefox (older version)
    - Google Chrome (older version)
    - Apple Safari (older version)
    - Damn Vulnerable Web Application (DVWA)

The following table provides the URLs from where we can download these software:

Software name	URL
VMware	http://www.vmware.com
Microsoft	http://www.microsoft.com
Ubuntu	http://www.ubuntu.com/
XAMMP	http://www.apachefriends.org/en/xampp-windows.html
Mozilla Firefox	https://www.mozilla.org/en-US/firefox/
Google Chrome	www.google.com/chrome
DVWA	www.dvwa.co.uk/

The following is a list of the hardware required:

- A PC based on CPU with two or more cores and at least 4 GB RAM
- ASUS WL-520gc (or similar) wireless router
- Any laptop as the attacker's host
- Any mobile device supporting Wi-Fi

Who this book is for

Instant Penetration Testing: Setting Up a Test Lab How-to is written those who only start to learn penetration testing and want to find the right way to start and improve their skills effectively.

Conventions

In this book, you will find a number of styles of text that distinguish between different kinds of information. Here are some examples of these styles, and an explanation of their meaning.

Code words in text are shown as follows: "By default, it is `admin:admin`."

A block of code is set as follows:

```
# Limit access to localhost
<Limit GET POST PUT>
order deny,allow
deny from all
allow from 127.0.0.1
</Limit>
```

Any command-line input or output is written as follows:

```
sudo apt-get -yu install vsftpd
```

New terms and **important words** are shown in bold. Words that you see on the screen, in menus or dialog boxes for example, appear in the text like this: "Click on **Apply**."

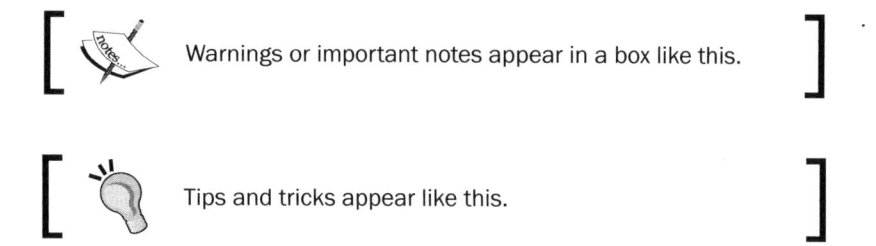

> Warnings or important notes appear in a box like this.

> Tips and tricks appear like this.

Reader feedback

Feedback from our readers is always welcome. Let us know what you think about this book—what you liked or may have disliked. Reader feedback is important for us to develop titles that you really get the most out of.

To send us general feedback, simply send an e-mail to `feedback@packtpub.com`, and mention the book title via the subject of your message.

If there is a book that you need and would like to see us publish, please send us a note in the **SUGGEST A TITLE** form on `www.packtpub.com` or e-mail `suggest@packtpub.com`.

If there is a topic that you have expertise in and you are interested in either writing or contributing to a book, see our author guide on `www.packtpub.com/authors`.

Customer support

Now that you are the proud owner of a Packt book, we have a number of things to help you to get the most from your purchase.

Errata

Although we have taken every care to ensure the accuracy of our content, mistakes do happen. If you find a mistake in one of our books—maybe a mistake in the text or the code—we would be grateful if you would report this to us. By doing so, you can save other readers from frustration and help us improve subsequent versions of this book. If you find any errata, please report them by visiting `http://www.packtpub.com/support`, selecting your book, clicking on the **errata submission form** link, and entering the details of your errata. Once your errata are verified, your submission will be accepted and the errata will be uploaded on our website, or added to any list of existing errata, under the Errata section of that title. Any existing errata can be viewed by selecting your title from `http://www.packtpub.com/support`.

Piracy

Piracy of copyright material on the Internet is an ongoing problem across all media. At Packt, we take the protection of our copyright and licenses very seriously. If you come across any illegal copies of our works, in any form, on the Internet, please provide us with the location address or website name immediately so that we can pursue a remedy.

Please contact us at `copyright@packtpub.com` with a link to the suspected pirated material.

We appreciate your help in protecting our authors, and our ability to bring you valuable content.

Questions

You can contact us at `questions@packtpub.com` if you are having a problem with any aspect of the book, and we will do our best to address it.

Instant Penetration Testing: Setting Up a Test Lab How-to

Welcome to *Instant Penetration Testing: Setting Up a Test Lab How-to*. This How-to contains the necessary information and essential steps required to do all the preparation work and build your own lab for practicing infrastructure, web, and Wi-Fi penetration testing.

Understanding penetration testing (Must know)

This section contains a short overview of penetration testing (what it is, what types of penetration testing exist, the typical workflow, and what you should remember).

Let us start by defining what penetration testing is and do a quick review of its main must-know details. According to *NIST SP 800-115, Technical Guide to Information Security Testing and Assessment*, it is defined as follows:

> *Penetration testing is security testing in which assessors mimic real-world attacks to identify methods for circumventing the security features of an application, system, or network. It often involves launching real attacks on real systems and data that use tools and techniques commonly used by attackers.*

Generally speaking, there are two main types of penetration tests:

- **External**: These tests are performed from the outside of the testing area (usually network) and mimicking potential external threats.
- **Internal**: These tests are performed from the inside of network and imitate a potential internal intruder, who could be a visitor (authorized or not) able to connect to the office network or a disloyal employee.

It is worth mentioning that external penetration tests could be additionally divided into several types by different criteria, sometimes based on targets:

- VPN penetration tests
- Web application penetration tests
- Wi-Fi penetration tests

It is important to say that penetration testing goals may vary as well. Some companies may want to check their network vulnerabilities, others may want to test the effectiveness of their security solutions such as IPS, and some may need to test their security processes such as monitoring and incident response. Moreover, there are also penetration tests necessary for compliance purposes; for example, PCI DSS. Those goals determine general conditions for penetration tests. Penetration tests are most-widely classified as follows:

- **Black box**: Penetration tester does not have any information about his targets prior to testing
- **Gray box**: Penetration tester has some basic information about target infrastructure
- **White box**: Penetration tester has all the information he needs and is able to ask the customer for additional info during the testing process

How to do it...

Everyone should know that the penetration testing workflow consists of the four following phases:

- Planning
- Discovery
- Attack
- Reporting

Planning and reporting phases are usually made once during the project, but discovery and attack phases could be iterated several times, depending on their results. The following is a diagram of the penetration testing workflow:

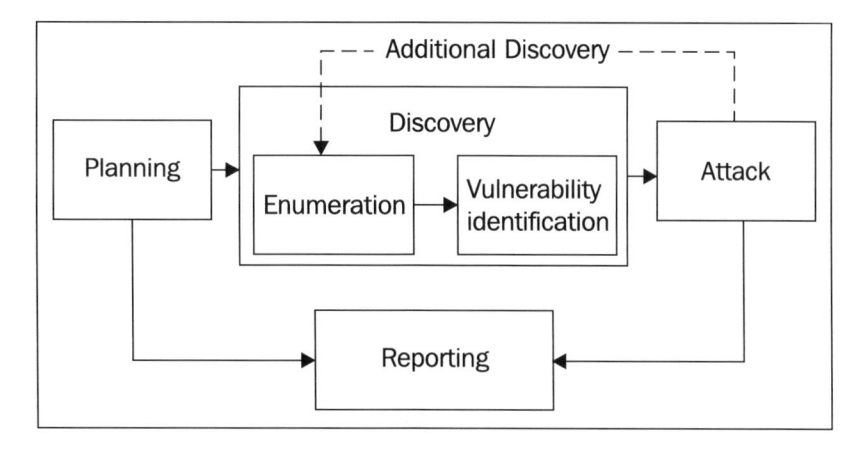

```
                    --- Additional Discovery -----
                    |                            |
                    |         Discovery          |
                    ↓                            |
┌──────────┐    ┌──────────────┬──────────────┐    ┌──────────┐
│ Planning │───▶│ Enumeration  │ Vulnerability│───▶│  Attack  │
│          │    │              │ identification│    │          │
└────┬─────┘    └──────────────┴──────────────┘    └────┬─────┘
     │                                                   │
     │              ┌─────────────┐                      │
     └─────────────▶│  Reporting  │◀─────────────────────┘
                    └─────────────┘
```

1. In the beginning, the planning phase, all the organizational questions are negotiated, all the approvals are received, the working time and dates are settled, and other management work is done. All this information will be used by a penetration tester in the reporting phase.

2. Discovery is the process of target networks and systems data mining (IPs, open ports, network services and versions, OSs, and so on) and vulnerability identification based on gained information. Data mining is performed by analyzing the target hosts' reactions and responses on external interaction. This interaction is often called **Enumeration** and could be performed by means of automated tools (scanning) or manually.

3. The next step after enumeration in the discovery phase is vulnerability identification. Similar to the enumeration process, this step could be automated, non-automated or, in most cases, mixed. The automated approach supposes the use of specialized software tools, while non-automated means comparing the targets' software versions gained during the enumeration process with vulnerability databases and analyzing the targets' behavior after data input.

   In general, different types of scanning are used simultaneously in the discovery phase, if there is no such goal to avoid IDS.

4. The next phase is actually penetration itself and is performed by conducting different kinds of attacks against disclosed vulnerabilities on target systems, which is called vulnerabilities exploitation. After a successful exploitation, you can get a new route to reach other systems, which were inaccessible before. In such cases, the penetration tester goes back to the discovery phase and repeats it for newly achieved targets. Thus, a couple of discovery and attack phases could be iterated several times, depending on the scope and agreements between a penetration tester and a client.

5. Finally, at the reporting phase, the penetration tester develops a final report, which includes all the organizational project details, all the data collected during the discovery phase, and a description of the attack phase with the obtained results.

There's more...

Here are some important things to remember.

Common reasons to set up your own lab

Before starting your work on planning and setting up the lab, it is a good idea to do some preparation work and determine your own reasons for why you need a lab. Normally, penetration testers and information security specialists have a combination of several reasons to build their own labs, but here I want to give you the most common reasons:

- It is the best way to practise professional penetration testing skills and gain more knowledge about testing
- All your practising in lab is legal, because you own and control it and there is no need to get a **Letter of Authorization** (**LOA**) first, so there is no risk of breaking the law
- This is a fully controlled environment, whose parameters and configurations could be changed in different ways in order to try different tools and techniques
- A lab could be useful for preparing a working environment; that is, configuring software tools and different templates in the laptop that will be used for penetration testing
- Using a fully controlled lab is one of the best ways to find and research new software vulnerabilities
- Information security mechanisms' and solutions' effectiveness and performance could also be researched and assessed in the lab

It is important to say that different types of penetration testing require different approaches and methodologies to be used for performing specific tasks. This is why a penetration tester has to work out all the basic methodologies step by step, permanently controlling everything that happens inside the lab environment and analyzing the environment reaction. This is why constant practising and learning are the two processes that are necessary for every professional penetration tester who wants to carry out projects successfully. You can use a lab, both for initial study with skill practising and for later training with penetration testing of certain technologies, or for learning new modes or functionality of your tools. The latter could be reached by setting up all appropriate technologies in your lab.

At the same time, if you are the penetration tester working with customers, you can meet a variety of different software and technologies used in the customer's networks and it is extremely important for you to be familiar with them and to know what to do. Also, during penetration tests, you might meet technologies, mechanisms, or software that are new for you. So, you obviously would have to learn and practise hacking them at a safe lab, but not on a customer's productive system.

On the other hand, if you are an information security officer or an internal penetration tester who is going to perform tests for your employer's company inside its corporate network, then you have to test the penetration testing methodology and plan its influence on target systems and the whole network (by means of training with your tools and researching), while not disrupting or reducing any system functionality or performance. On the basis of the results of such a training, a penetration tester can usually tune specific tools or choose tools that work with the target environment in the most effective way.

What is more important is that the speed and effectiveness of the whole penetration testing process often depends upon how good and comfortable tools are set up in pentesting laptop. However, just installing all the necessary tools is not enough – laptop tuning and hardening is another significant activity in preparation for performing penetration tests. Consequently, the lab becomes very useful for writing most common scripts, configuring proxies and frameworks, identifying network connection parameters, and so on.

I also mentioned that using your own lab is also a good way to find and research new software vulnerabilities. A lot of information security researchers use their own labs for this reason. In general, the research process usually includes the following steps:

1. Installing the interested software that needs to be researched.
2. Using special techniques to find vulnerabilities; for example, fuzzing.
3. Using a debugger or other techniques to research vulnerability and determine its parameters.
4. Understanding the possible effects of vulnerability exploitation.
5. Creating and testing **Proof-of-Concept** (**PoC**) for this vulnerability to publicly demonstrate that it is exploitable.

The last reason for setting up your own lab that I would like to mention, is assessing the effectiveness and performance of information security mechanisms and solutions. In this case, a lab is useful because you can research the behavior of security facilities by sequentially applying different attack techniques on them and varying configuration parameters. One of the important advantages of using a lab for such assessments is the ability to legally and safely perform stress-testing of information systems and security facilities.

What you should remember

There are several important rules that you should always remember in order to avoid law infringement while performing penetration testing:

> To avoid any legal problems, you should always get an approval from your customers. LOA is an authoritative permission, which makes penetration test legal. LOA should be issued by the proper authorities, very specifically in scope (actually, what to test) of penetration testing and must contain confirmation from the customer, who he really owns all assets in the scope.

- Like in every information security audit or assessment, you should also negotiate a **Non-Disclosure Agreement** (**NDA**) with the customer prior to starting your penetration test project. This agreement limits the information disclosure for both sides, so customers are confident in saving the confidentiality of their information, and you are certain about your methodology privacy.
- It is important to negotiate organizational details such as specific testing windows (exact dates and time), necessary contacts, and incident response procedures in case of an accidental target system failure.

Additional reading

If you want to go deeper into the penetration testing process and its details, you can check the following:

- *NIST SP 800-115, Technical Guide to Information Security Testing and Assessment*
- *Hacking Exposed 7: Network Security Secrets & Solutions*, by *Stuart McClure, Joel Scambray*, and *George Kurtz, 2012*
- `http://www.pentest-standard.org`

Planning the lab environment (Should know)

This section reveals how to plan your lab environment step by step and shows what you should consider during the lab planning process.

Getting ready

To get the best result after setting up your lab, you should plan it properly at first. Your lab will be used to practise certain penetration testing skills. Therefore, in order to properly plan your lab environment, you should first consider which skills you want to practise based on ideas and reasons listed in the *Understanding penetration testing (Must know)* recipe. Although you could also have non-common or even unique reasons to build a lab, I can provide you with the average list of skills one might need to practice:

- Essential skills
    - Discovery techniques
    - Enumeration techniques
    - Scanning techniques
    - Network vulnerability exploitation
    - Privilege escalation
    - OWASP TOP 10 vulnerabilities discovery and exploitation
    - Password and hash attacks
    - Wireless attacks

- Additional skills
    - Modifying and testing exploits
    - Tunneling
    - Fuzzing
    - Vulnerability research
    - Documenting the penetration testing process

All these skills are applied in real-life penetration testing projects, depending on its depth and the penetration tester's qualifications. The following skills could be practised at three lab types or their combinations:

- Network security lab
- Web application lab
- Wi-Fi lab

I should mention that the lab planning process for each of the three lab types listed consists of the same four phases:

1. **Determining the lab environment requirements**: This phase helps you to actually understand what your lab should include. In this phase, all the necessary lab environment components should be listed and their importance for practising different penetration testing skills should be assessed.
2. **Determining the lab environment size**: The number of various lab environment components should be defined in this phase.
3. **Determining the required resources**: The point of this phase is to choose which hardware and software could be used for building the lab with the specified parameters and fit it with what you actually have or are able to get.
4. **Determining the lab environment architecture**: This phase designs the network topology and network address space.

How to do it...

Now, I want to describe step by step how to plan a common lab combined of all three lab types listed in the preceding section using the following four-phase approach:

Instant Penetration Testing: Setting Up a Test Lab How-to

1. **Determine the lab environment requirements**:

    To fit our goal and practise particular skills, the lab should contain the following components:

Skills to practise	Necessary components
Discovery techniques	Several different hosts with various OSs
Enumeration techniques	
Scanning techniques	Firewall
Network vulnerability exploitation	IPS
OWASP TOP 10 vulnerabilities discovery and exploitation	Web server
	Web application
	Database server
	Web application firewall
Password and hash attacks	Workstations
	Servers
	Domain controller
	FTP server
Wireless attacks	Wireless router
	Radius server
	Laptop or any other host with Wi-Fi adapter
Modifying and testing exploits	Any host
	Vulnerable network service
	Debugger
Privilege escalation	Any host
Tunneling	Several hosts
Fuzzing	Any host
Vulnerability research	Vulnerable network service
	Debugger
Documenting the penetration testing process	Specialized software

Now, we can make our component list and define the importance of each component for our lab (importance ranges between less important, **Additional,** and most important, **Essential**):

Components	Importance
Windows server	Essential
Linux server	Important
FreeBSD server	Additional
Domain controller	Important
Web server	Essential
FTP Server	Important
Web site	Essential
Web 2.0 application	Important
Web application firewall	Additional
Database server	Essential
Windows workstation	Essential
Linux workstation	Additional
Laptop or any other host with Wi-Fi adapter	Essential
Wireless router	Essential
Radius server	Important
Firewall	Important
IPS	Additional
Debugger	Additional

2. **Determine the lab environment size:**

   In this step, we should decide how many instances of each component we need in our lab. We will count only the essential and important components' numbers, so let's exclude all additional components. This means that we've now got the following numbers:

Components	Number
Windows server	2
Linux server	1
Domain controller	1
Web server	1

Components	Number
FTP Server	1
Web site	1
Web 2.0 application	1
Database server	1
Windows workstation	2
Host with Wi-Fi adapter	2
Wireless router	1
Radius server	1
Firewall	2

3. **Determine required resources**:

    Now, we will discuss the required resources:

    - Server and victim workstations will be virtual machines based on VMWare Workstation 8.0. To run the virtual machines without any trouble, you will need to have an appropriate hardware platform based on a CPU with two or more cores and at least 4 GB RAM.
    - Windows servers OSs will work under Microsoft Windows 2008 Server and Microsoft Windows Server 2003.
    - We will use Ubuntu 12.04 LTS as a Linux server OS. Workstations will work under Microsoft Windows XP SP3 and Microsoft Windows 7.
    - ASUS WL-520gc will be used as the LAN and WLAN router.
    - Any laptop as the attacker's host.
    - Samsung Galaxy Tab as the Wi-Fi victim (or other device supporting Wi-Fi).

    We will use free software as a web server, an FTP-server, and a web application, so there is no need for any hardware or financial resources to get these requirements.

4. **Determine the lab environment architecture**:

    Now, we need to design our lab network and draw a scheme:

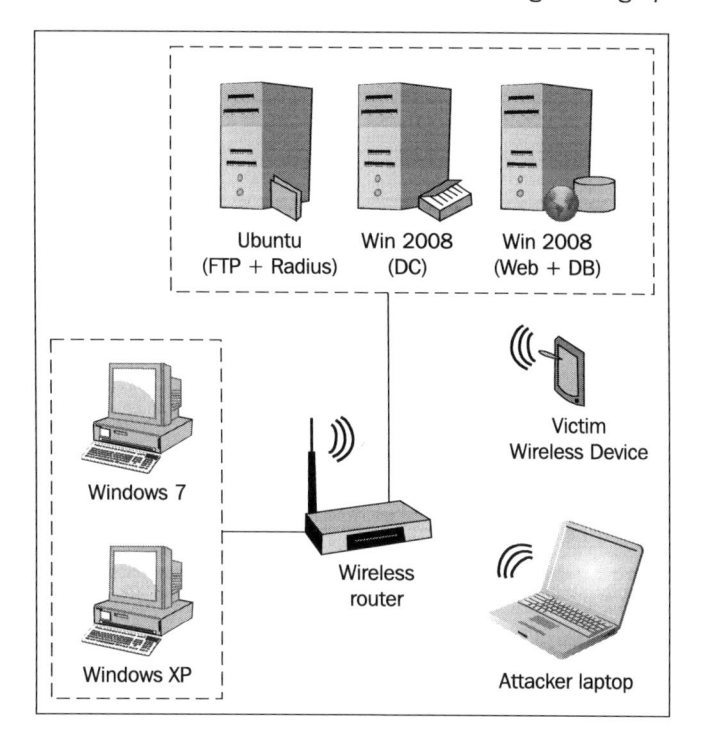

Address space parameters:

- **DHCP server**: 192.168.1.1
- **Gateway**: 192.168.1.1
- **Address pool**: 192.168.1.2-15
- **Subnet mask**: 255.255.255.0

How it works...

In the first step, we discovered which types of lab components we need by determining what could be used to practise the following skills:

- All OSs and network services are suitable for practising discovery, enumeration, and scanning techniques and also for network vulnerability exploitation. We also need at least two firewalls – windows built-in software and router built-in firewall functions.

- Firewalls are necessary for learning different scanning techniques and firewall rule detection knowledge. Additionally, you can use any IPS for practising evasion techniques.

- A web server, a website, and a web application are necessary for learning how to disclose and exploit OWASP TOP 10 vulnerabilities. Though a **web application firewall** (**WAF**) is not necessary, it helps to improve web penetration testing skills to a higher level.
- An FTP service ideally serves as a way to practise password brute-forcing. Microsoft domain services are necessary to understand and try Windows domain passwords and hash attacks including relaying. This is why we need at least one network service with remote password authentication and at least one Windows domain controller with two Windows workstations.
- A wireless access point is essential for performing various wireless attacks, but it is better to combine a LAN router and Wi-Fi access point in one device. So, we will use a Wi-Fi router with several LAN ports. A radius server is necessary for practising attacks on WLAN with WPA-Enterprise security.
- A laptop and a tablet PC with any Wi-Fi adapters will work as an attacker and victim in wireless attacks.
- Tunneling techniques could be practised at any two hosts; it does not matter whether we use Windows or any other OS.
- Testing and modifying exploits as well as fuzzing and vulnerability research need a debugger installed on a vulnerable host.
- To properly document a penetration testing process, one can use just any test processor software, but there are several specialized software solutions, which make things much more comfortable and easier.

In the second step, we determined which software and hardware we can use as instances of chosen component types and set their importance based on a common lab for a basic and intermediate professional level penetration tester.

In the third step, we understood which solutions will be suitable for our tasks and what we can afford. I have tried to choose a cheaper option, which is why I am going to use virtualization software. The ASUS WL-520gc router combines the LAN router and Wi-Fi access point in the same device, so it is cheaper and more comfortable than using dedicated devices. A laptop and a tablet PC are also chosen for practising wireless attacks, but it is not the cheapest solution.

In the fourth step, we designed our lab network based on determined resources. We have chosen to put all the hosts in the same subnet to set up the lab in an easier way. The subnet has its own DHCP server to dynamically assign network addresses to hosts.

There's more...

Let me give you an account of alternative ways to plan the lab environment details.

Lab environment components variations

It is not necessary to use a laptop as the attacker machine and a tablet PC as the victim – you just need two PCs with connected Wi-Fi adapters to perform various wireless attacks.

As an alternative to virtual machines, a laptop, and a tablet PC or old unused computers (if you have them) could also be used to work as hardware hosts. There is only one condition – their hardware resources should be enough for planned OSs to work.

An IPS could be either a software or hardware, but hardware systems are more expensive. For our needs, it is enough to use any freeware Internet security software including both the firewall and IPS functionality.

It is not essential to choose the same OS as I have chosen in this chapter; you can use any other OSs that support the required functionality. The same is true about network services – it is not necessary to use an FTP service; you can use any other service that supports network password authentication such as telnet and SSH.

You will have to additionally install any debugger on one of the victim's workstations in order to test the new or modified exploits and perform vulnerability research, if you need to.

Finally, you can use any other hardware or virtual router that supports LAN routing and Wi-Fi access point functionality. A connected, dedicated LAN router and Wi-Fi access point are also suitable for the lab.

Choosing virtualization solutions – pros and cons

Here, I want to list some pros and cons of the different virtualization solutions in table format:

Solution	Pros	Cons
VMWare ESXi	▶ Enterprise solution ▶ Powerful solution ▶ Easily supports a lot of virtual machines on the same physical server as separate partitions ▶ No need to install the OS	▶ Very high cost ▶ Requires a powerful server ▶ Requires processor virtualization support

Solution	Pros	Cons
VMWare workstation	▶ Comfortable to work with ▶ User friendly GUI ▶ Easy install ▶ Virtual *nix systems work fast ▶ Better works with virtual graphics	▶ Shareware ▶ It sometimes faces problems with USB Wi-Fi adapters on Windows 7 ▶ Demanding towards system resources ▶ Does not support 64-bit guest OS ▶ Virtual Windows systems work slowly
VMWare player	▶ Freeware ▶ User-friendly GUI ▶ Easy to install	▶ Cannot create new virtual machines ▶ Poor functionality
Micrisoft Virtual PC	▶ Freeware ▶ Great compatibility and stability with Microsoft systems ▶ Good USB support ▶ Easy to install	▶ Works only on Windows and only with Windows ▶ Does not support a lot of features that concurrent solutions do
Oracle Virtual Box	▶ Freeware ▶ Virtual Windows systems work fast ▶ User-friendly GUI ▶ Easy to install ▶ Works on Mac OS and Solaris as well as on Windows and Linux ▶ Supports the "Teleportation" technology	▶ Paid USB support ▶ Virtual *nix systems work slowly

Here, I have listed only the leaders of the virtualization market in my opinion. Historically, I am mostly accustomed to VMWare Workstation, but of course, you can choose any other solutions that you may like.

You can find more comparison info at `http://virt.kernelnewbies.org/TechComparison`.

Setting up the network security lab (Must know)

This section is aimed at setting up a lab environment for practising penetration testing in general. Skills that you can practise with this type of lab are as follows:

- Essential skills
    - Discovery techniques
    - Enumeration techniques
    - Scanning techniques
    - Network vulnerability exploitation
    - Privilege escalation
    - Password and hash attacks

- Additional skills
    - Modifying and testing exploits
    - Tunneling
    - Fuzzing
    - Vulnerability research
    - Documenting the penetration testing process

Getting ready

Prior to setting up the network security lab environment, let's do some preparation. We need to clearly understand our lab network topology for this task. It will differ from the topology given in the *Planning the lab environment (Should know)* recipe, because of tweaking for the current lab needs. In this recipe, the other components are necessary:

- Router
- Domain controller (Windows 2008)
- FTP server (Ubuntu)
- Two workstations (Windows 7 Pro and Windows XP Pro)
- Attacker workstation

Instant Penetration Testing: Setting Up a Test Lab How-to

You can see the current task network topology in the following diagram:

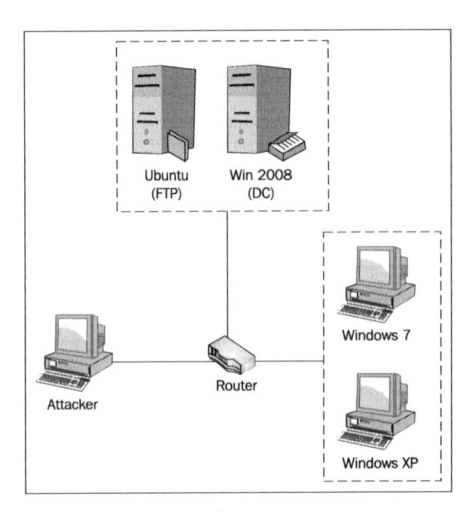

Since we decided to use virtual machines, we need to clearly understand the current lab environment architecture (physical and logical). One physical PC will be used as a host workstation for virtual machines. It could be the same PC, which will be used as an attacker workstation. One more physical component is the router; all other components will be virtual machines, bridged to the router via a host workstation network interface. The described network security lab architecture is provided in the following diagram:

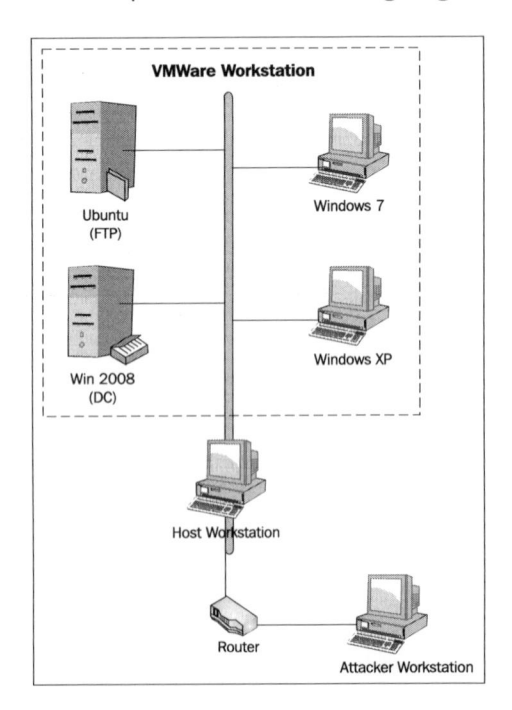

Before we proceed with setting up the lab, you should prepare the router and distributions of the following software:

- VMware Workstation 8 (installer)
- Microsoft Windows Server 2008 (`.iso` installer disk image)
- Ubuntu server 12 (`.iso` installer disk image)
- Windows 7 (`.iso` installer disk image)
- Windows XP (`.iso` installer disk image)

Except VMware Workstation, software versions without service packs are preferable, because they contain more publicly announced vulnerabilities, which you can exploit to practise your skills in the lab.

How to do it...

We need to configure our router in the first step. For my example, I used ASUS WL-520GC, but the difference between home routers is not significant:

1. Plug in the power supply and Internet connection cable to the router. The Internet connection cable should be plugged in the WAN port.
2. Now, connect the LAN adapter of the computer, which will host the virtual machines (host workstation) to any of the router LAN ports with the network cable.
3. The power indicator, WAN port indicator, and one of LAN port indicators in the router front panel must shine with green lights.
4. Open the browser on the host workstation, go to the address `192.168.1.1`, and input the username and password for the router. By default, it is `admin:admin`.
5. In the left panel, click on the IP **config** link and input your WAN settings (taken from your ISP) to the corresponding fields. Leave the LAN IP settings as default (IP: `192.168.1.1`, Subnet Mask: `255.255.255.0`). Click on **Apply**.
6. In the **DHCP Server** page, enable **Integrated DHCP server** and change the setup of the IP pool from `192.168.1.2` to `192.168.1.15`. Click on **Apply**.
7. Go to the Internet firewall section, enable **Internet firewall** and disable **Web access from WAN**. All other settings are left by default. Click on **Finish** and then **Save & Restart**.
8. The router will reboot, which indicates that it is ready for us to work with it.

Instant Penetration Testing: Setting Up a Test Lab How-to

Now, we need to install our virtualization software; in my case, it is VMware Workstation 8 (the installation process is similar for older versions):

1. Start the setup process by executing the distribution file.
2. Choose the custom setup type and click on **Next** to view the setup options:

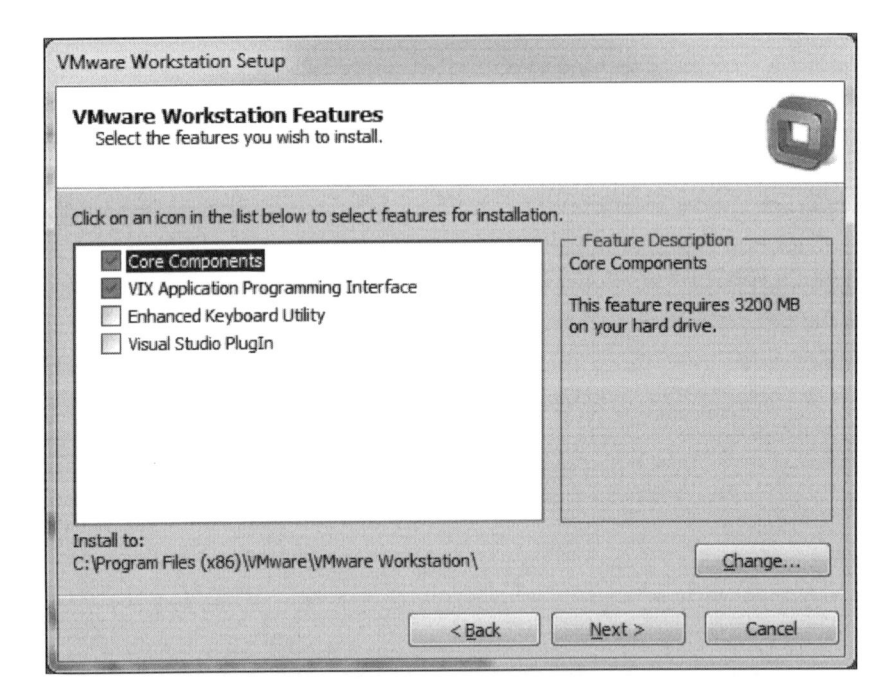

3. I used the default settings, which are enough for our task, but you can change them if you need more VMware features enabled or want to install it into another directory. After selecting your settings, click on **Next**.
4. Select the **Check for product updates on startup** checkbox on the next screen and click on **Next**.
5. Select the **Help improve VMware Workstation** checkbox on the next screen if you want to let the VMware Workstation software send the debugging information to VMware company servers for further analysis. Click on **Next**.
6. Select the location where you want to put shortcuts for VMware Workstation, and click on **Next**.
7. Click on **Continue** to start the installation process. It can take a while to install the program and its components.
8. Enter your license key when prompted for it, and finish the installation.

Now, we need to update the VMware Workstation software to the latest version:

1. Run VMware Workstation.
2. In the drop-down menu **Help**, click on **Software Updates**.
3. In the opened **Software Updates** windows, click on the **Check for Updates** button.
4. Install the available updates by choosing them and click on **Next**.

Now, the VMware workstation is ready for work and we can proceed with the other lab components.

First, we should install the servers. Let us start from Windows Server 2008 which will be our DC.

1. Select **New virtual machine...** in the drop-down menu **File of VMware Workstation** or press *Ctrl + N*.
2. In the opened wizard, select the typical configuration for the new virtual machine and click on **Next**.
3. In the next window, select **Installer disk image file (iso)**, and browse through the path to the installer image of Windows Server 2008, and click on **Next**:

23

4. In the next window, type in a product key if you have one or skip it, select the **Windows Server 2008 Enterprise** version, type in the user name (I use `lab` here), and click on **Next**:

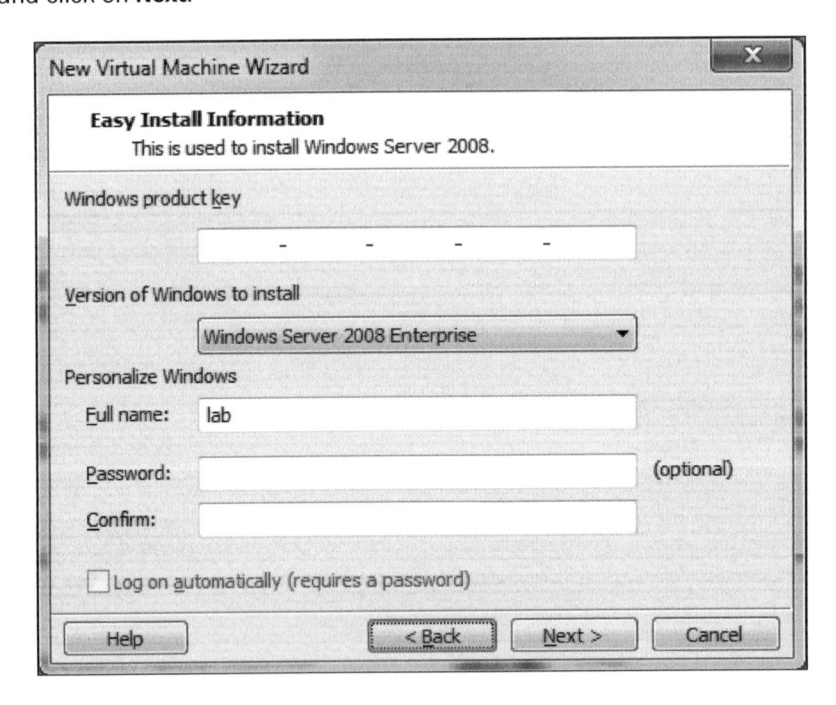

If you did not provide a product key, a new dialog window will appear and ask for your confirmation in order to proceed without a product key. Click on **Yes**.

5. In the next window, type in the name for this virtual machine (I used the default one). Choose the file location for the virtual machine path and click on **Next**:

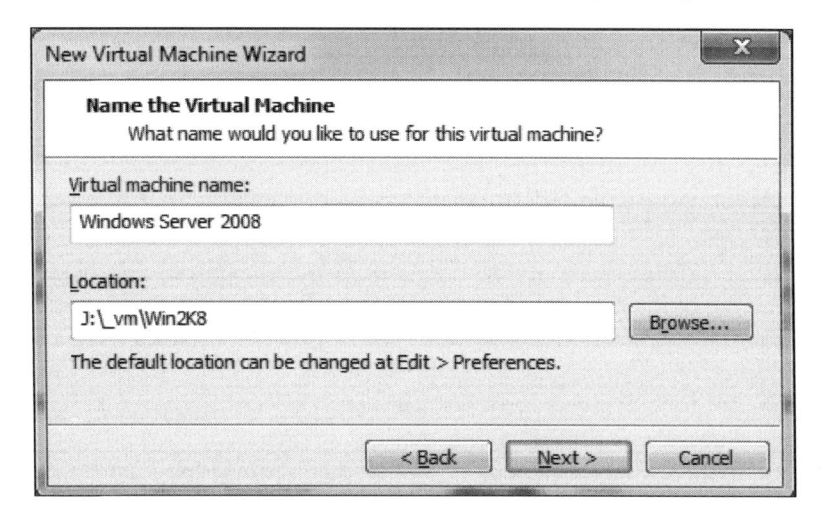

Instant Penetration Testing: Setting Up a Test Lab How-to

[New Virtual Machine Wizard dialog: Name the Virtual Machine — Virtual machine name: Windows Server 2008; Location: J:_vm\Win2K8]

6. Set the system volume disk size for the virtual machine (it is better to set no less than 40 gigabytes) in the next window and select **Split virtual disk into multiple files**, then click on **Next**.

7. Click on the **Customize hardware** button in the next window to manually set virtual machine hardware parameters.

8. In the new window, set no less than 1 GB of memory, but it's better to set 2 GB or more. Set the essential parameters to the following values:

Parameter	Value
Memory	2 GB
Processors	1
Network adapter	Bridged (without physical network connection state replication)
USB controller	None
Display	Use host settings for monitors

Instant Penetration Testing: Setting Up a Test Lab How-to

9. Click on **Close**.
10. Select **Power on this virtual machine after creation** and click on **Finish**.
11. Now, your virtual machine is ready for installing the OS. This process will start automatically after turning the virtual machine on and will last for a while.
12. The VMware workstation will automatically start installing the VMware tools after the installation of the Windows 2008 server; wait until this process ends.
13. Reboot the guest system and log in. You must see the initial configuration dialog box.
14. Click on the **Set time zone** link and set your time, date, and time zone.
15. Provide a computer description and the name using the link in the initial configuration window.
16. Open the **Local area connection properties** window using the following sequence: **Configure networking | Local area connection | Properties**. Leave all properties to the default setting except TCP/IPv4. Set the values for the TCP/IPv4 properties as shown in the following screenshot:

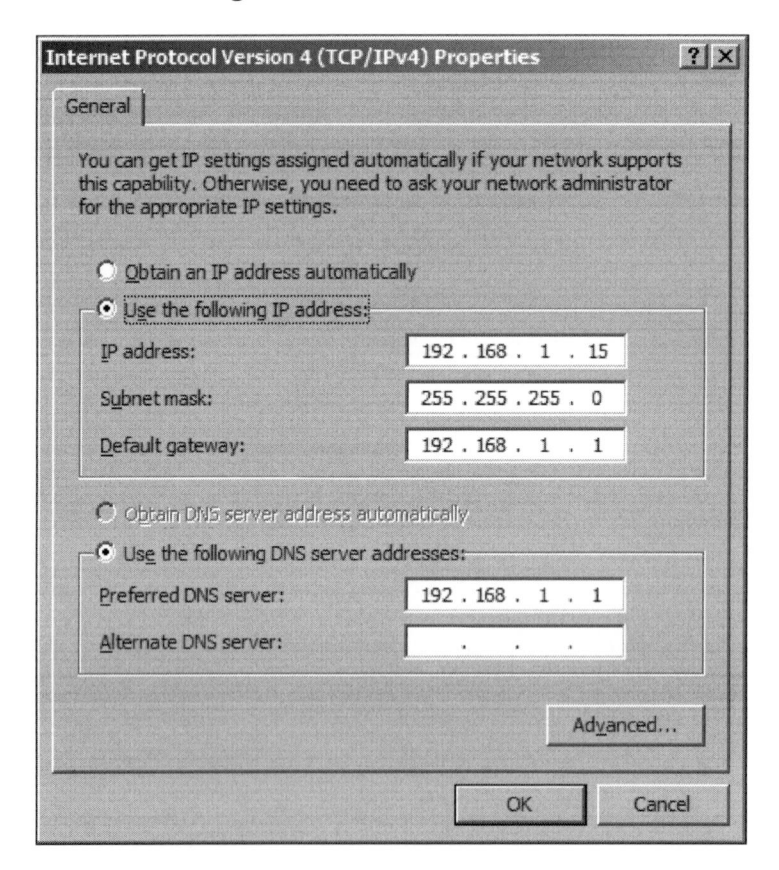

Now, you should have an initial configuration window similar to the following screenshot:

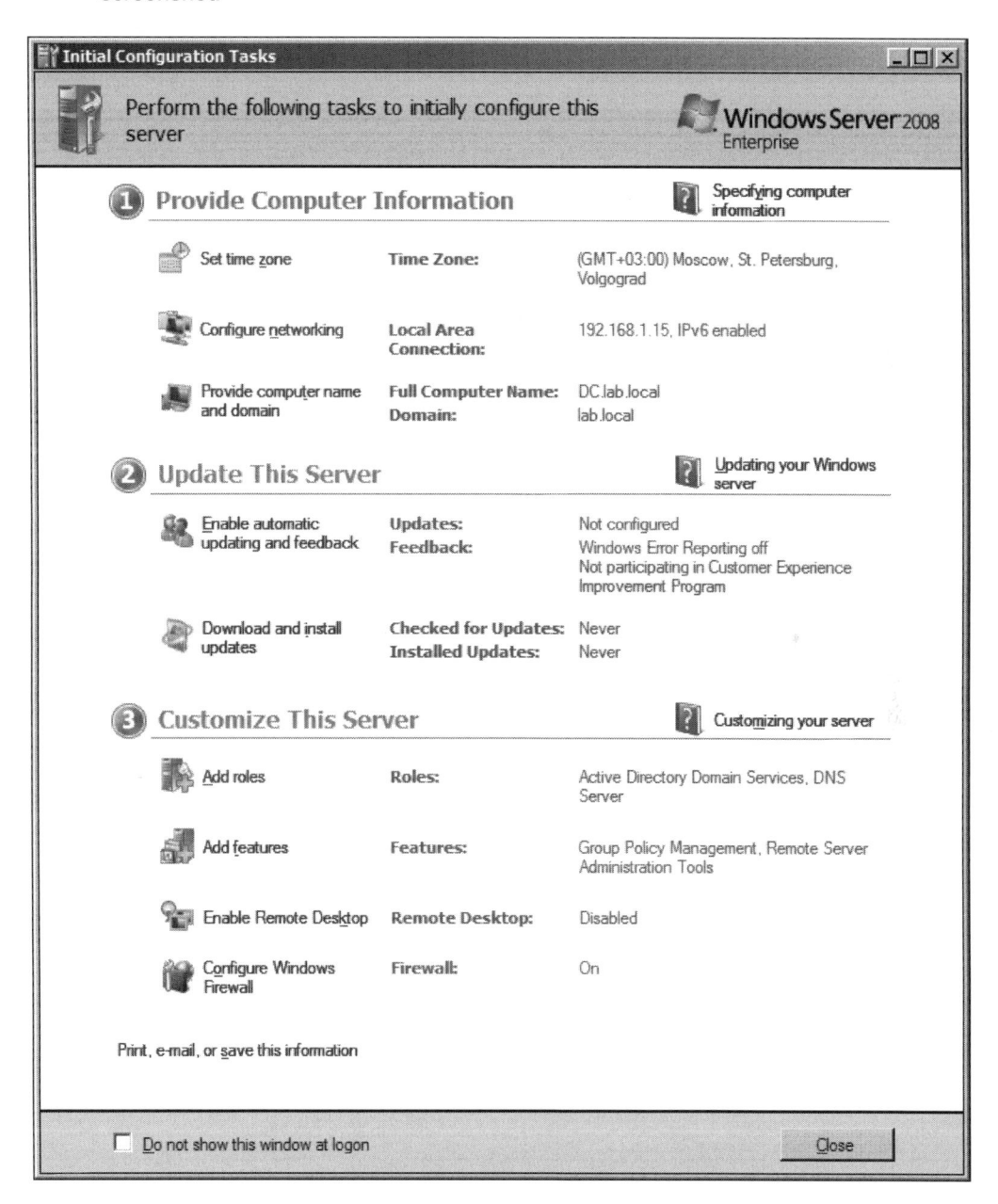

![Initial Configuration Tasks window for Windows Server 2008 Enterprise showing Provide Computer Information (Time Zone: (GMT+03:00) Moscow, St. Petersburg, Volgograd; Local Area Connection: 192.168.1.15, IPv6 enabled; Full Computer Name: DC.lab.local; Domain: lab.local), Update This Server (Updates: Not configured; Feedback: Windows Error Reporting off, Not participating in Customer Experience Improvement Program; Checked for Updates: Never; Installed Updates: Never), and Customize This Server (Roles: Active Directory Domain Services, DNS Server; Features: Group Policy Management, Remote Server Administration Tools; Remote Desktop: Disabled; Firewall: On).]

17. Now, we need to assign a Domain Controller role to our server. In the initial configuration window, click on the **Add roles** link and then **Next** to open the **Server Roles** assigning dialog window. Select the **Active Directory Domain Services** checkbox and start the role installation by clicking on the **Next** and **Install** buttons:

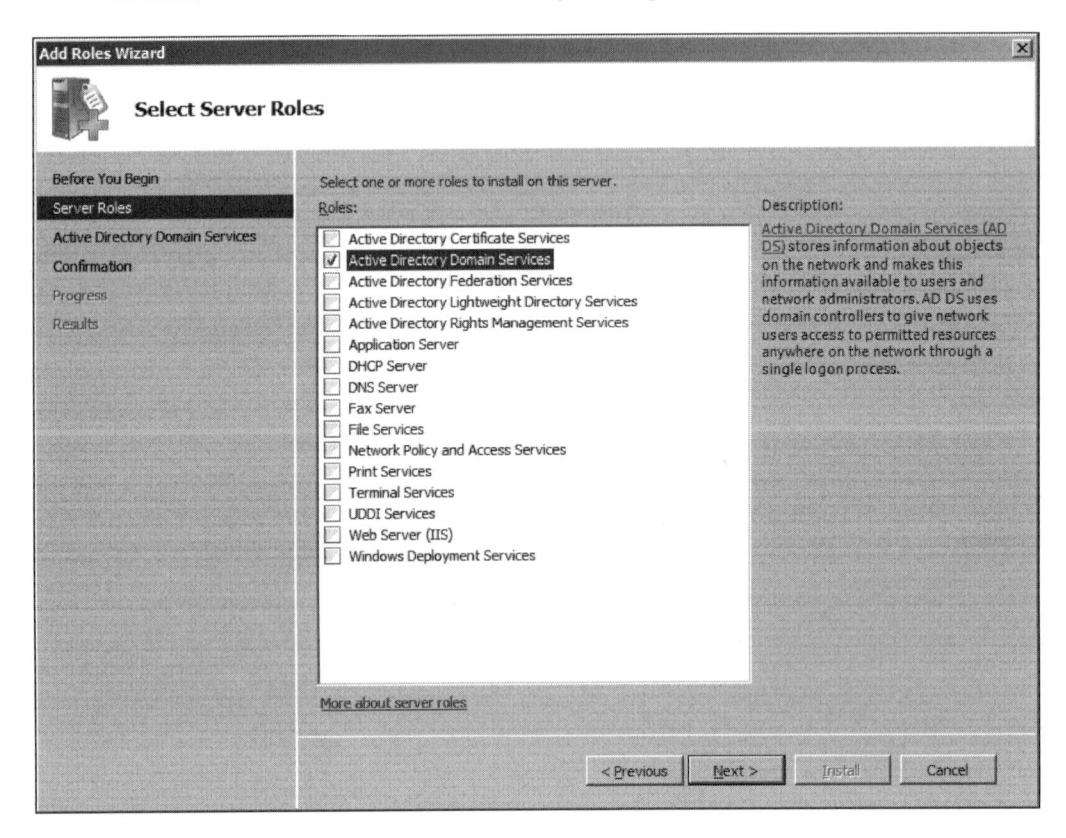

18. When the role installation will be finished, open the **Start** menu and type in `dcpromo` in the **Search** field. Launch **dcpromo**:

19. Continue clicking on **Next** in the opened dialog window until you get to the **Choosing deployment configuration** dialog box, select **Create a new domain in a new forest**, and click on **Next**:

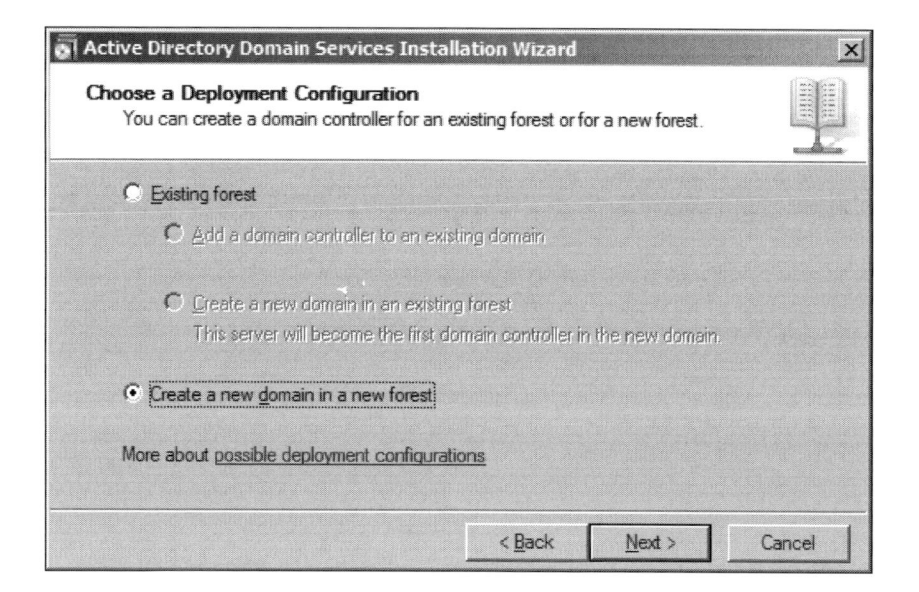

Instant Penetration Testing: Setting Up a Test Lab How-to

20. Type in your lab domain name (FQDN), for example `lab.local`, and click on **Next**:

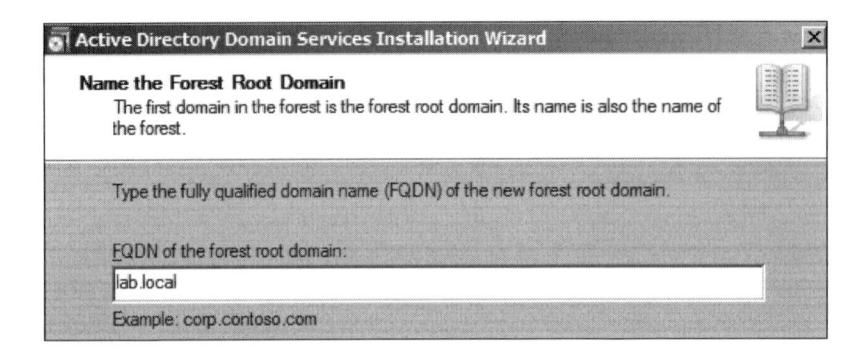

21. Now, we need to choose the functional level for the domain forest. Choose the latest version in your system (for mine, it is **Windows Server 2008**) and click on **Next**:

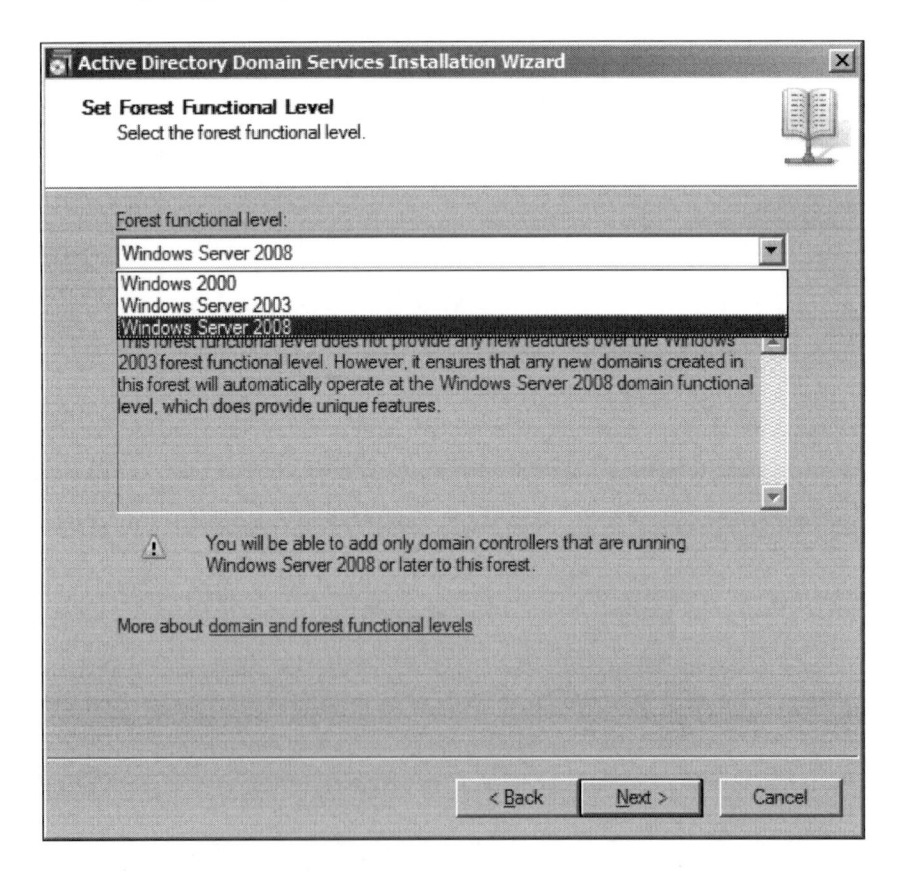

22. In the next screen, we must enable a **DNS server** role for our domain controller in order for it to work correctly:

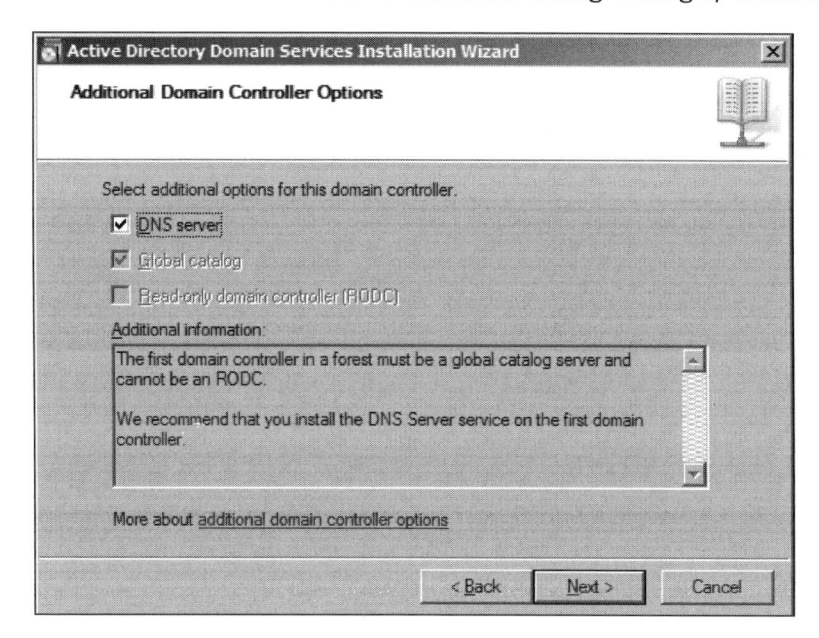

23. When the wizard prompts you about the integration with an existing DNS infrastructure, click on **Yes**.
24. In the next dialog box, leave the `Database`, `Log`, and `SYSVOL` folders as default and click on **Next**.
25. Set the directory service restore mode administrator account password and click on **Next**.
26. Check the summary info, click on **Next**, wait while the wizard is installing active directory domain services, and restart the system.
27. Take a snapshot of the domain controller virtual machine after its successful installation and initial configuration. To take a snapshot, select the **Take Snapshot** menu item, type in a snapshot name and comments in the dialog window, and click on the **Take Snapshot** button:

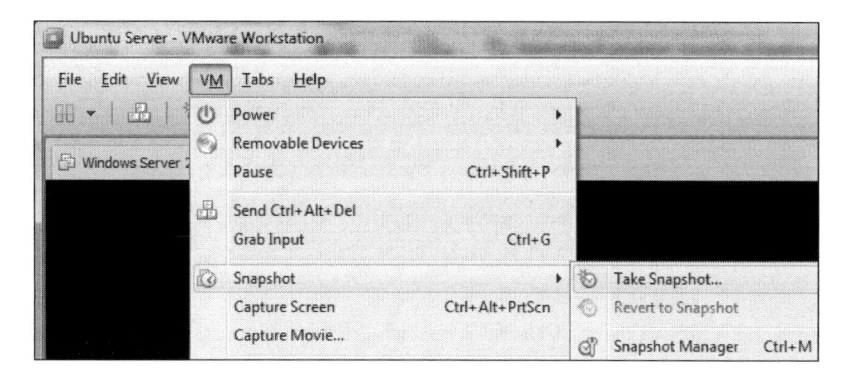

After creating a domain controller, continue with installing Ubuntu Server:

1. In VMware Workstation press *Ctrl + N* and follow the on-screen instructions to create a new Ubuntu virtual machine. This process is similar to creating a Windows Server 2008 virtual machine, so you should not have any trouble. Make sure you do not forget the root password that you enter during this process and set the network connection as bridged.

2. Ubuntu installation will start automatically after finishing with virtual machine creation. It will also automatically install VMware tools. It will take several minutes depending on your computer's performance and virtual machine properties.

3. After the installation, you should be able to see a standard Ubuntu Server console with a login invitation:

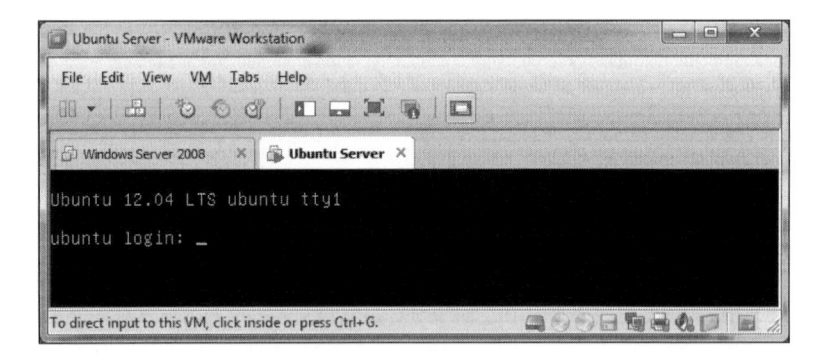

4. Log in and type the `ifconfig` command without arguments to find the name of your network interface. In my case it is `eth0`.

5. Now, configure your network interface by executing the following command:

   `sudo ifconfig eth0 192.168.1.14 netmask 255.255.255.0 broadcast 192.168.1.255`

   You will have to type in the root password to execute the command. After this, check if network interface settings are set as per our requirements, by typing the `ifconfig` command again but without any argument:

6. Now, we need to add a route through a default gateway in order to let our server access the Internet. Do it by executing the following command:

```
sudo route add default gateway 192.168.1.1
```

7. Now, execute the `route` command without any arguments and try `ping www.google.com`:

   ```
   lab1@ubuntu:~$ sudo route add default gateway 192.168.1.1
   lab1@ubuntu:~$ route
   Kernel IP routing table
   Destination     Gateway         Genmask         Flags Metric Ref    Use Iface
   default         my.router       0.0.0.0         UG    0      0        0 eth0
   192.168.1.0     *               255.255.255.0   U     0      0        0 eth0
   lab1@ubuntu:~$ ping www.google.com
   PING www.l.google.com (74.125.232.51) 56(84) bytes of data.
   64 bytes from www.google.com (74.125.232.51): icmp_req=1 ttl=57 time=11.4 ms
   64 bytes from www.google.com (74.125.232.51): icmp_req=2 ttl=57 time=11.7 ms
   ^C
   --- www.l.google.com ping statistics ---
   2 packets transmitted, 2 received, 0% packet loss, time 1001ms
   rtt min/avg/max/mdev = 11.440/11.610/11.781/0.201 ms
   ```

8. Let us install the FTP server now. I have chosen `vsftpd` as the solution for an easy way to install and setup. Type in the following command:

   ```
   sudo apt-get -yu install vsftpd
   ```

   The installation will be done in automated mode.

9. To configure the `vsftp` daemon, open the `/etc/vsftpd.conf` file with the Nano editor by executing the following command:

   ```
   sudo nano /etc/vsftpd.conf
   ```

10. Uncomment the following lines in the `vsftpd.conf` file:

    ```
    local_enable=YES
    ```

    ```
    write_enable=YES
    ```

11. Then, press *Ctrl + X* to exit. Answer Y to the question about saving your changes and choose the same file for saving `/etc/vsftpd.conf`.

12. Now, we need to create at least one user who will have FTP access to his home directory. The easiest way to do it is to use the `adduser` command, which will prompt you with all the needed data and automatically create the user's home directory:

    ```
    lab1@ubuntu:~$ sudo adduser ubuntu_user
    Adding user `ubuntu_user' ...
    Adding new group `ubuntu_user' (1001) ...
    Adding new user `ubuntu_user' (1001) with group `ubuntu_user' ...
    Creating home directory `/home/ubuntu_user' ...
    Copying files from `/etc/skel' ...
    Enter new UNIX password:
    Retype new UNIX password:
    passwd: password updated successfully
    Changing the user information for ubuntu_user
    Enter the new value, or press ENTER for the default
            Full Name []:
            Room Number []:
            Work Phone []:
            Home Phone []:
            Other []:
    Is the information correct? [Y/n] y
    lab1@ubuntu:~$
    ```

13. Restart the FTP daemon by executing the following command:
    ```
    sudo /etc/init.d/vsftpd restart
    ```
14. Take a snapshot of your new virtual Ubuntu server.

Now, we need to install and set up virtual Windows workstations. Let's start from Windows XP:

1. In VMware Workstation, press *Ctrl + N* and follow the on-screen instructions to create a new virtual machine with customized parameters. Do not forget to set up the network interface for the virtual machine as `bridged`. The Windows XP installation process starts automatically right after creating a virtual machine.

2. You will be prompted to enter the Windows product key if you have not done it in the previous step. Enter the valid product key (you can find a lot of trial keys on the Internet). Windows XP with SP3 lets you skip the product key entering step during installation.

3. As long as we use virtual machines for our lab, performance is important for us. We can improve the performance of Windows XP in the following ways:

    1. Open **Control Panel** from the **Start** menu and switch to the classic view.
    2. Double-click on the **System** icon.
    3. Go to the **Advanced** tab and click on the **Settings** button in the **Performance** section.
    4. Select the **Adjust to best performance** option and click on **Apply and OK**:

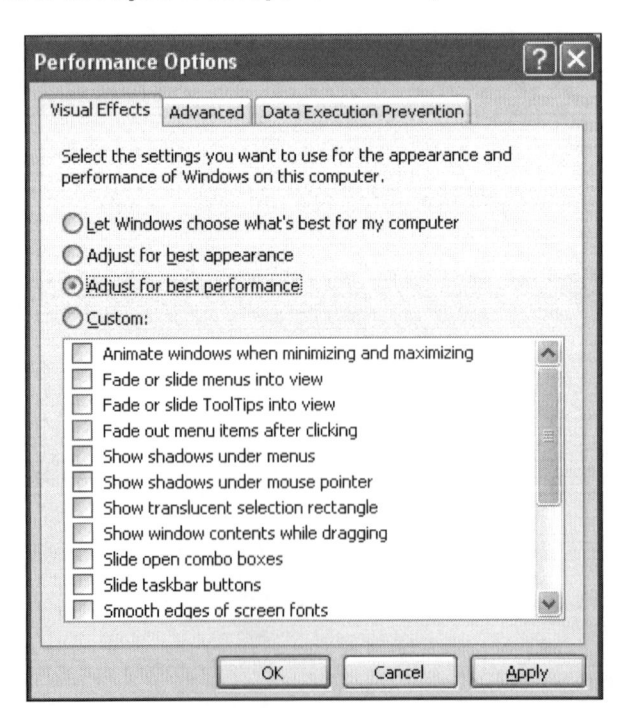

Instant Penetration Testing: Setting Up a Test Lab How-to

4. As this workstation will be used to practice penetration testing skills, it should have some vulnerabilities. This is why we need to turn off automatic updates — go to the **Automatic Updates** tab, select **Turn Off Automatic updates**, and click on **Apply** and then **OK**.

5. The network connection for the Windows XP workstation is configured to acquire the dynamic IP address by default, so it must be already set. But, you need to manually set the domain controller IP as the primary DNS server address:

    1. Open **Control Panel** and double-click on the **Network connections** icon.
    2. Open **Local Area Connection** and its properties.
    3. Select **Internet Protocol (TCP/IP)** and click on the **Properties** button.
    4. Set the following properties and return to **Control Panel**:

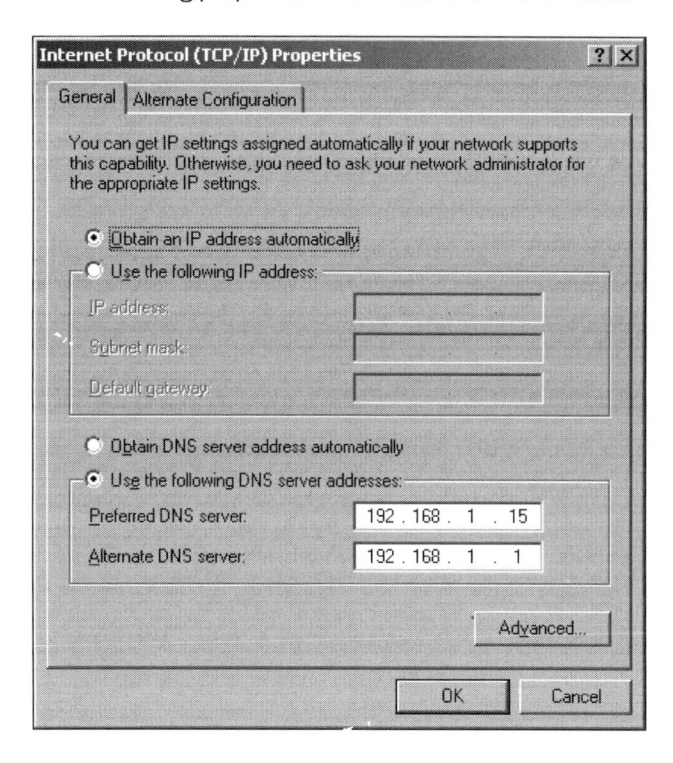

6. Now, we need to join the Windows XP workstation to our lab domain:

    1. Make sure that the domain controller is turned on.
    2. Double-click on the **System** icon.
    3. Go to the **Computer Name** tab in the **System Properties** dialog window.
    4. Click on the **Change...** button.
    5. Set the computer name as `WinXP`.

6. In the **Member of** section, select the **Domain** radio button and type in the lab domain name in the text field below it. In my case, it is `lab.local`, and click on **OK**:

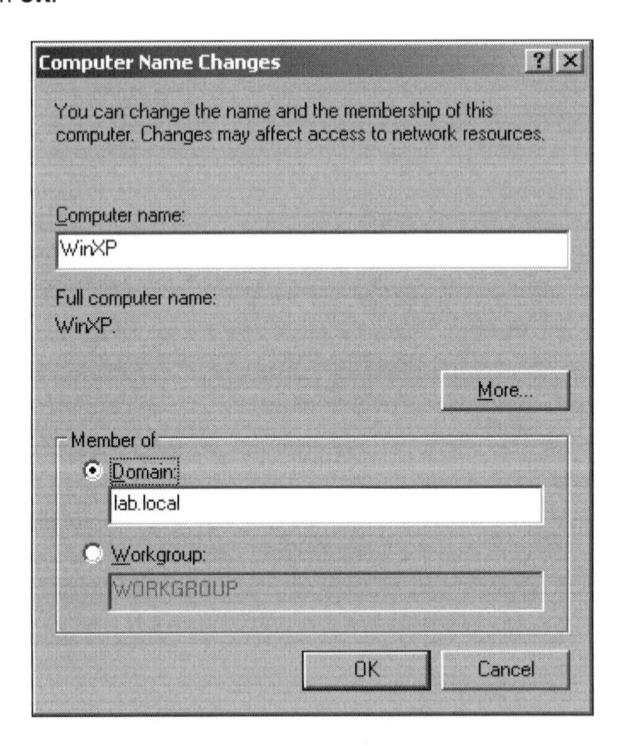

7. You will be prompted for domain credentials. Enter the domain administrator's credentials and you should see the welcome window.

7. Restart the Windows XP virtual machine and take a snapshot of it.

The last lab component is Windows 7:

1. In VMware Workstation, press *Ctrl + N* and follow the on-screen instructions to create a new virtual machine with customized parameters. Do not forget to set up the network interface for the virtual machine as `bridged`. The Windows 7 installation process starts automatically right after creating a virtual machine.

2. Windows 7 starts automatically after its installation.

3. Log in and set up the performance setting to **Adjust for best performance** in the **System Properties** dialog window; it can be found at **Control Panel | All Control Panel Items | System | Advanced System Settings**.

4. Turn to the **Computer Name** tab and join this workstation to the lab domain in the same way as we did for Windows XP.

5. Reboot the system and take a snapshot.

Instant Penetration Testing: Setting Up a Test Lab How-to

Finally, we are done with the installation and configuration tasks and can check some components to see if they work ok:

1. By joining the Windows workstation to the domain, we have already checked if the lab domain works.
2. Now, check the FTP server in the following way:
    1. In the Windows XP **Start** menu, find the **Run** command and enter `cmd`.
    2. In the command line, type `ftp` and press *Enter*.
    3. Type the command `open 192.168.1.14` and press *Enter*.
    4. You should see something similar to the following code if the FTP server works:

       ```
       Connected to 192.168.1.14.
       220 (vsFTPd 2.3.5)
       User (192.168.1.14:(none)):
       ```
    5. Enter the username and password.
    6. After logging in, enter the `ls` command and the `ftp` user directory listing should be executed if everything works fine.
3. Try to ping all the hosts from every host.

How it works...

Let's explore the essential steps that we just went over.

During the router configuration process, we need to restrict Internet users from rooting our lab router, so we should disable web access to the router from the external network (WAN) and activate the firewall.

When you start the VMware Workstation software, it will indicate if there are any updates available, and will ask if you want to install them. Some updates need to uninstall VMware Workstation first to install the new version. It will be done automatically if you click on **Yes**. Software updates for VMware Workstation are strongly recommended to be installed, because it is a way to fix known bugs and security flaws in VMware software.

But, we do not need any software updates for our virtual systems because we need them to have vulnerabilities with which we can practice penetration testing skills. This is the reason why I recommend you to turn off the automatic updates on all virtual systems.

We use bridged network interfaces in our virtual machines in order to let them communicate with the router, as they were physical hosts. If we set up NAT, then our systems will use VMware Workstation as a software DHCP server and will work in another subnet than the router.

I intentionally did not type in the Windows product key, because I use it only for demonstration purposes less than 30 days. But if you want to use it longer, then I recommend you to buy licenses.

The domain controller as well as DNS server; should have a static IP address in order to operate well. So, let it be `192.168.1.15`. It is also a good practice to give static IPs to servers; that is why our Ubuntu server also has a static IP.

A domain infrastructure needs a DNS server that is why we used `dcpromo` to install a DNS server role to the domain controller for maintaining the active directory.

During the domain controller configuration process, I set only two roles (**Domain Services** and **DNS Server**), but you can add or remove other roles for any training purposes and at any time later.

By default, `vsftpd` is configured to only allow an anonymous download. During the installation, an FTP user is created with a home directory `/home/ftp`. This is the default FTP directory. But we want to practise password guessing techniques with the FTP server, so we need to create different FTP users. I have shown you how to create an FTP user and now you can easily create as many users as you want.

There's more...

Being a professional penetration tester means always going further find out more information than was given and constantly improving your knowledge. This is common for both a professional penetration tester and a real hacker, and this is also the reason to check the next paragraphs.

Alternative solutions and configurations

You have to understand that the described way of building a network security lab is not the only one or the right one – there could be plenty of variations and different solutions starting from small personal labs to corporate virtualization clusters.

Let me give you some options:

- If you are going to research vulnerabilities and modify or write your own exploits, it might be useful to set up VMware Workstation with the Visual Studio plugin for debugging purposes. It provides an interface between virtual machines and Microsoft Visual Studio.
- You may need to add other hosts and install other additional network services in order to practise specific skills. This is not difficult, and you can always find appropriate manuals on the Internet.
- You can also replace some or all of the virtual machines with old unused physical computers and connect them into a network with a router or switch.

- If you do not want to manually install and configure all virtual systems, you can find virtual machines with already installed OSs on the Internet. You can also use specially-crafted vulnerable virtual machines. For example, one of the best vulnerable machines for lab purposes is **Metasploitable**.

Additional tips

Here, I would like to tell you about some more useful things:

- After setting up the lab and taking snapshots of all the virtual machines, you will start performing different kinds of techniques and attacks against them. When you finish with the basic discovery and enumeration attacks, you would probably want to improve your skills to the next level and test yourself against different security solutions. In that case, install and set up integrated **host antivirus**, **firewall**, and **intrusion preventing systems** (**HIPS**) on the target virtual machines and take new snapshots. This will let you practise different firewall rules enumeration techniques, which is called **firewalking**, and different IDS evasion techniques. You can always revert your systems from any state to any of your snapshots in order to compare the results of using different techniques performed on different system states.

- One of the most useful techniques that I usually use during penetration testing projects is tunneling. It is a technique for passing your traffic through hosts, already controlled by you (successfully attacked). This means that you can reach non-routable hosts and networks. That is why I strongly recommend you to learn and practise it in your lab if you want to leverage your penetration testing skills robustly.

- Always try new techniques and software in your lab to understand them well.

- Try different penetration testing distributions such as BackTrack, and choose which fits you the best.

- I always take snapshots of my virtual systems. A snapshot is a saved state of a virtual machine that lets you return to any point you have previously saved. This means that you have a great opportunity to do whatever you want with your virtual machines, without being afraid of totally misconfiguring or losing them. So, do not forget to take snapshots.

Additional info

To get additional info, you can check the following resources:

- `technet.microsoft.com`
- `www.ubuntu.com`
- `www.offensive-security.com` and `www.offensive-security.com/metasploit-unleashed/Metasploitable`
- `www.backtrack-linux.org`
- `pentestlab.wordpress.com`

Instant Penetration Testing: Setting Up a Test Lab How-to

Setting up a web app lab (Should know)

This section is aimed at setting up a lab environment for practising web application penetration testing. You can practise the following skills using this type of a lab:

- Essential skills
    - Enumeration techniques
    - Scanning techniques
    - OWASP TOP 10 vulnerabilities discovery and exploitation
    - Privilege escalation
- Additional skills
    - Fuzzing
    - Vulnerability research
    - Documenting the penetration testing process

Getting ready

At first, we have to determine the web app lab topology and architecture. In this recipe, we will use only components essential for web app penetration testing and will not include others. The following lab components are necessary for our current task:

- Router
- Web server
- Victim web client workstation
- Attacker workstation

You can see the current task network topology in the following diagram:

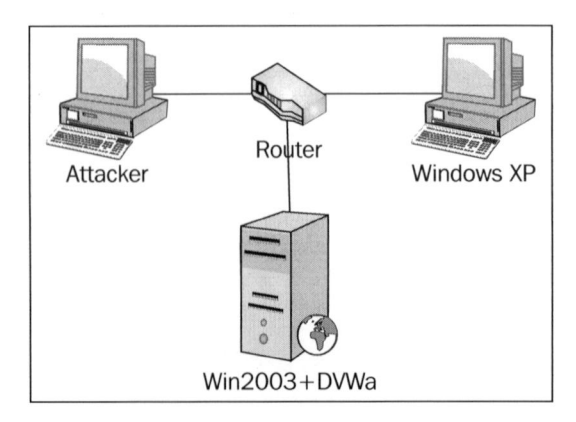

Instant Penetration Testing: Setting Up a Test Lab How-to

Our lab topology and physical architecture will not be the same as we are going to build the lab on virtual machines. We will use one physical router and one physical PC (which will also be an attacker's host) for hosting a virtual web server, and a virtual client workstation with bridged network interfaces.

The described network security lab architecture is provided in the following diagram:

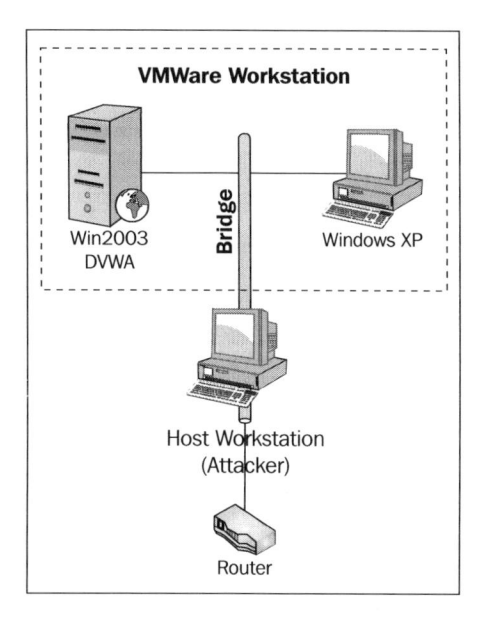

VMWare Workstation

Win2003 DVWA — Bridge — Windows XP

Host Workstation (Attacker)

Router

Before we proceed with setting up the lab, you should prepare the router and distributions of the following software:

- VMware Workstation 8 (installer)
- Microsoft Windows Server 2003 (.iso installer disk image)
- Windows XP (.iso installer disk image)
- XAMPP Apache distribution (installer for Windows can be downloaded from http://www.apachefriends.org/en/xampp-windows.html)
- Mozilla Firefox (offline installer, the older the version, the better it is)
- Google Chrome (offline installer, the older the version, the better it is)
- Apple Safari (offline installer, the older the version, the better it is)

Except VMware Workstation, older software versions and no service packs are preferable, because they contain more publicly announced vulnerabilities, which you can exploit to practise your skills in the lab.

I recommend finding the offline browser installer, otherwise installers will try to download and install the latest versions with fixed bugs.

Instant Penetration Testing: Setting Up a Test Lab How-to

How to do it...

As always, our initial steps should be configuring the router and installing the VMware Workstation 8 in the same way as it was described in the *Setting up the network security lab (Must know)* recipe.

After updating the VMware Workstation, you can disconnect the WAN cable from your router as we do not need an Internet connection anymore.

Now, we can proceed with setting up a web client workstation and a web server hosting a vulnerable web application. Let us start with a workstation. It will be the Windows XP workstation with several web browsers installed:

1. In the VMware Workstation, press *Ctrl + N* and follow the on-screen instructions to create a new virtual machine with customized parameters. Do not forget to set up the network interface for a virtual machine as `bridged`. The Windows XP installation process starts automatically right after creating a virtual machine.

2. You will be prompted to enter the Windows product key if you have not done it in the previous step. Enter the valid product key (you can find a lot of trial keys on the Internet). Windows XP, with SP3, lets you skip the product key entering step during installation.

3. So long as we use virtual machines for our lab, performance is important for us. We can improve the performance of Windows XP in the following way:

    1. Open **Control Panel** through the **Start** menu and switch to the classic view.
    2. Double-click on the **System** icon.
    3. Go to the **Advanced** tab and click on the **Settings** button in the **Performance** section.
    4. Select the **Adjust to best performance** option and click on **Apply and OK**.

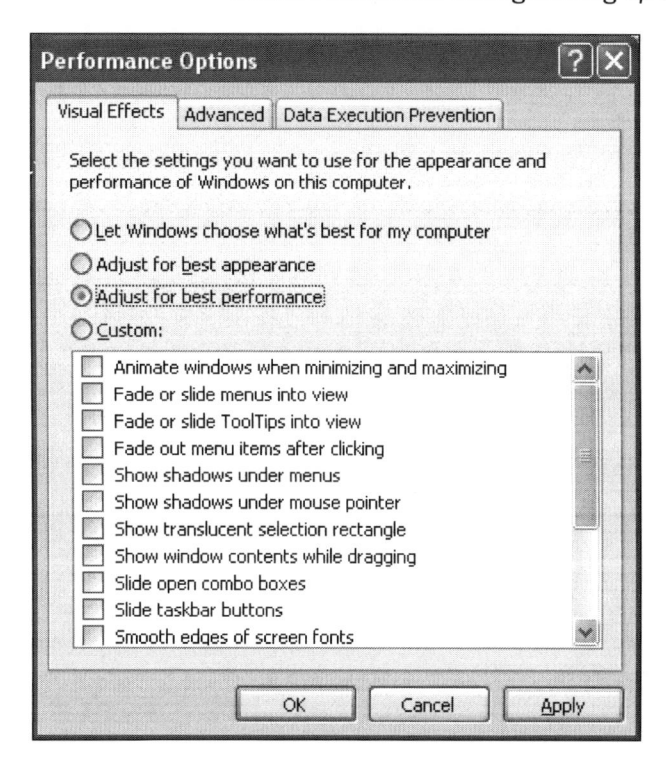

4. As this workstation will be used to practise penetration testing skills, it should have some vulnerabilities. This is why we need to turn off automatic updates; go to the **Automatic Updates** tab, select the **Turn Off Automatic updates** option, and click **Apply** and then **OK**.

5. The network connection for the Windows XP workstation is configured to acquire a dynamic IP address by default, so it must be already set. But, you need to manually set the domain controller IP as the primary DNS server address:

    1. Open **Control Panel** and double-click on the **Network connections** icon.
    2. Open **Local Area Connection** and its properties.

Instant Penetration Testing: Setting Up a Test Lab How-to

3. Select **Internet Protocol (TCP/IP)** and click on the **Properties** button.

4. Set up the following properties and return to the **Network connections** window:

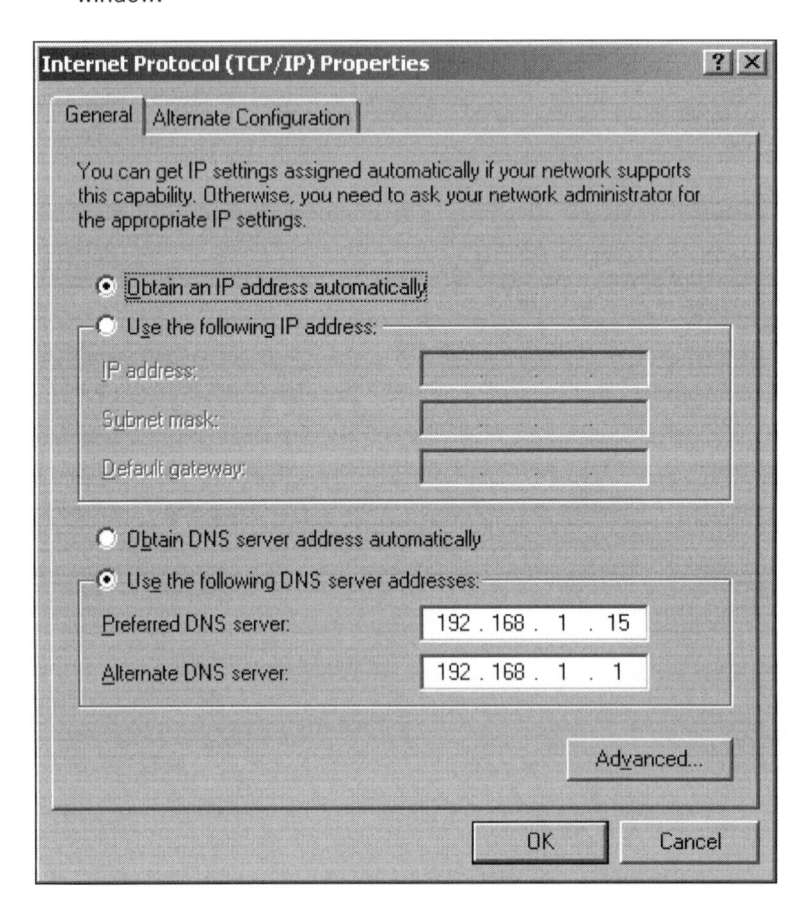

![Internet Protocol (TCP/IP) Properties dialog showing "Obtain an IP address automatically" selected, "Use the following DNS server addresses" selected with Preferred DNS server 192.168.1.15 and Alternate DNS server 192.168.1.1]

6. We need to turn the network interface off before installing browsers so they do not download and install the latest versions. Right-click on **Local Area Connection** and select **Disable**:

The network connection icon should become grey, which means an inactive state of the interface.

7. Install the Google Chrome browser (for the web app lab's needs, I use Chrome v.14) by running the installer and following the on-screen instructions.
8. Now, we need to turn off the Google Chrome automatic updates. In the **Start** menu click on **Run** and enter the `regedit` command.
9. Find the `HKEY_LOCAL_MACHINE\SOFTWARE\Policies` key in the registry editor.
10. Create a subkey `\Google\Update\`.
11. In `HKEY_LOCAL_MACHINE\SOFTWARE\Policies\Google\Update\`, create a DWORD parameter `AutoUpdateCheckPeriodMinute`, and set its value to `0`:

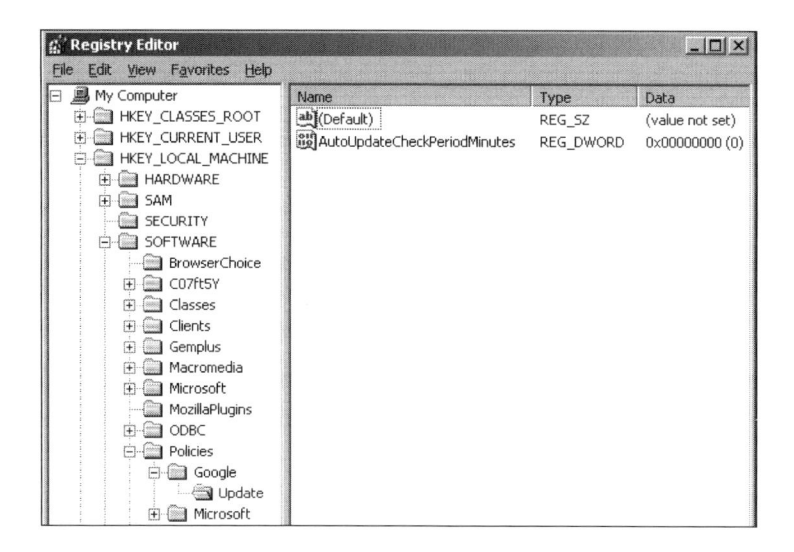

12. Close the registry editor and run the Mozilla Firefox installer (for the web app lab's needs, I use Firefox v8).
13. Follow the on-screen instructions and select **Standard Installation**.
14. Run the Mozilla Firefox browser after the installation.
15. Select the option not to import any data from other browsers when prompted.
16. In the **Tools** drop-down menu, select **Options**.
17. Go to the **Advanced** tab in the **Options** window.
18. Open the sub-tab **Update** and deselect all the checkboxes. For Firefox 8, it looks similar to the following screenshot:

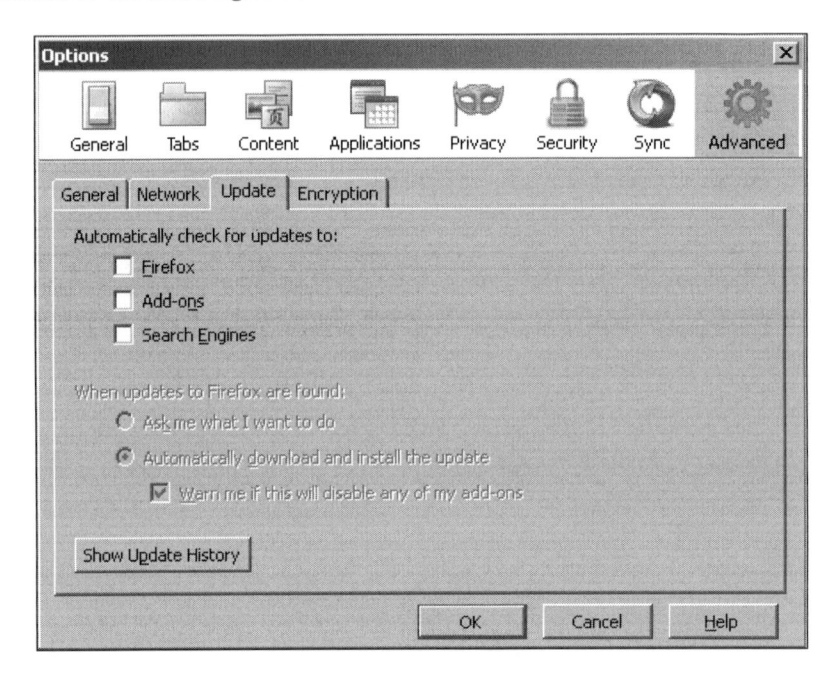

For the latest versions of Firefox, for example 15, the update options sub-tab has been changed and you need to select **Never check for updates**, as shown in the following screenshot:

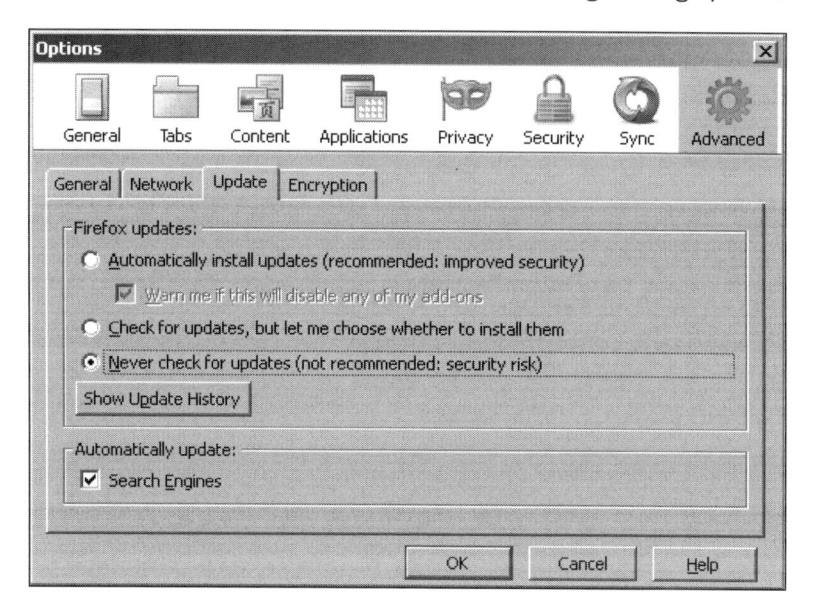

Instant Penetration Testing: Setting Up a Test Lab How-to

19. Close Mozilla Firefox and proceed with installing the Apple Safari browser.
20. Run the Apple Safari installer (for the web app lab's needs, I use Safari v4), and follow the on-screen instructions.
21. Apple Safari lets you choose the automatic update options during installation, so deselect the **Automatically update Safari and other Apple software** checkbox when prompted, and finish the installation.
22. Now, open the **Network Connections** window from **Control Panel** and enable **Local Area Connection** by right-clicking on its icon and selecting **Enable**:

23. The last thing we need to do with our Windows XP virtual machine is take a snapshot.
24. In the VM dropdown menu of VMware Workstation, select **Snapshot | Take Snapshot...**, and input a name and a description for the new snapshot:

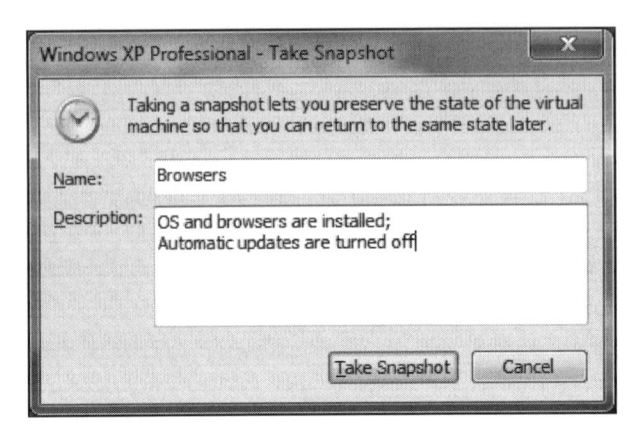

Our web client workstation is now ready for lab experiments, and we can go further by installing a Windows 2003-based web server.

25. In VMware Workstation, press *Ctrl + N*, and follow the on-screen instructions to create a new virtual machine with customized parameters. Do not forget to set up the network interface for the virtual machine as `bridged`.
26. Depending on the Windows Server 2003 distribution, the installer can prompt you with which type of Windows 2003 you want to install. We need to choose **Windows 2003 Server Standard** (option **B**):

27. After this, the Windows Server 2003 installation process starts.
28. During the installation, you will be prompted for a product key. Enter any trial key found on the Internet or enter a valid key if you have a license.
29. After the installation of Windows Server 2003, wait until VMware Tools is installed and restart the system.
30. Now, we need to set up the network connection properties. Open **Local Area Connection Properties** and set the static IP `192.168.1.13` using other IP settings, as described in the *Setting up the network security lab (Must know)* recipe.
31. Now, copy the XAMPP installer to the Windows 2003 Server virtual machine and run it.

32. Follow the on-screen instructions and leave the XAMPP path by default as `C:\xampp\` when prompted:

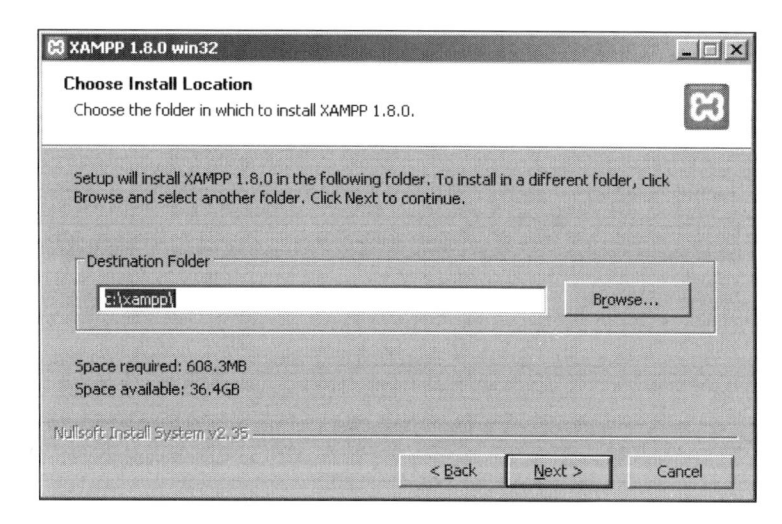

33. Also, we should install Apache and MySQL as services, so select the following checkboxes during installation:

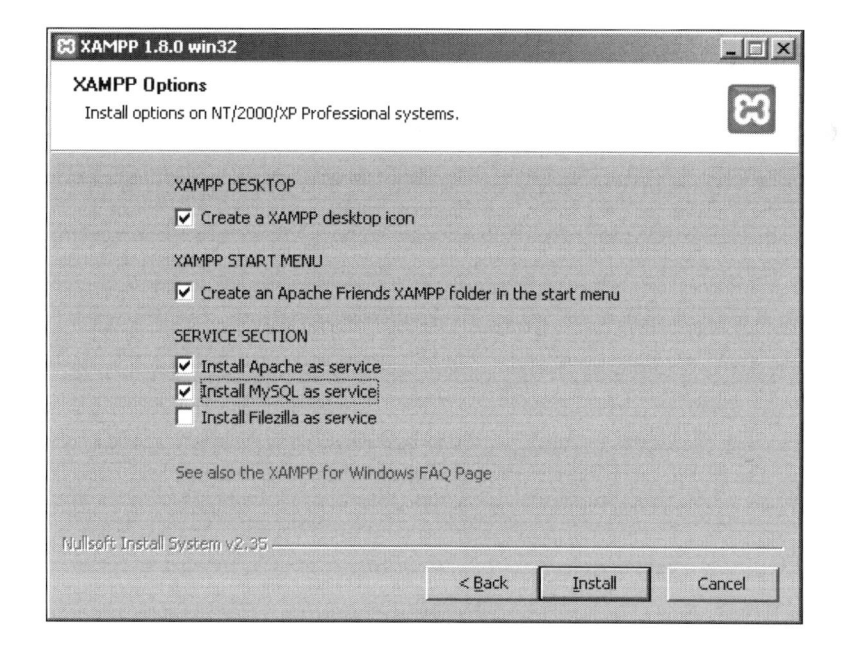

34. Click on **Install** and wait while the installation ends.
35. The Apache server and the MySQL server will start automatically after the installation.

Instant Penetration Testing: Setting Up a Test Lab How-to

36. Now, find the `htdocs` directory in the `XAMPP` directory (in my case, it is `C:\xampp\htdocs`), and delete all the default content from that directory:

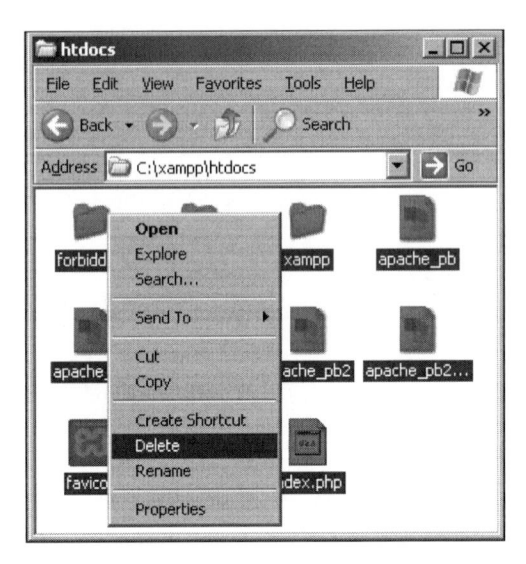

37. Now, copy the unzipped Damn Vulnerable Web Application folder `dvwa` into the empty `htdocs` directory.
38. Go to the `dvwa` directory and find the `.htaccess` file.
39. Open it for editing with notepad.
40. Find the next part of the code:

    ```
    # Limit access to localhost
    <Limit GET POST PUT>
    order deny,allow
    deny from all
    allow from 127.0.0.1
    </Limit>
    ```

41. Replace it with the following:

    ```
    # Limit access to localhost
    <Limit GET POST PUT>
    order deny,allow
    #deny from all
    #allow from 127.0.0.1
    allow from all
    </Limit>
    ```

42. Save the file and close the Notepad.

43. Let us now simplify the attacker's task by reducing some PHP security settings. Go to the XAMPP control panel, click on Apache's **Config** button and select **PHP (php.ini)** to open the PHP `config` file:

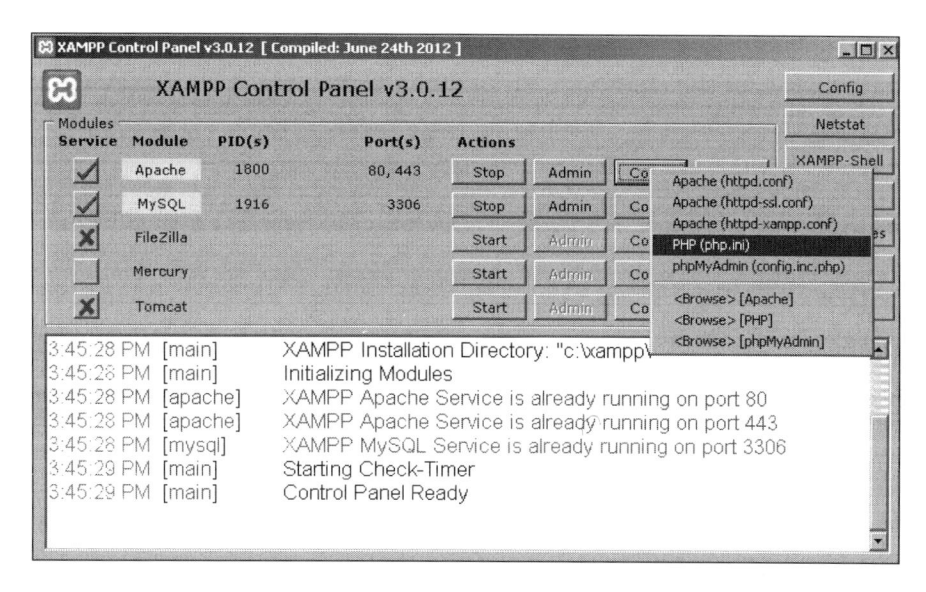

44. Find the `allow_url_fopen` parameter in the `php.ini` file and set its value to `off`.
45. Find the `allow_url_include` parameter and set its value to `off` as well.
46. Now, we need to restart the Apache server to apply the new settings. Click on Apache's **Stop** button:

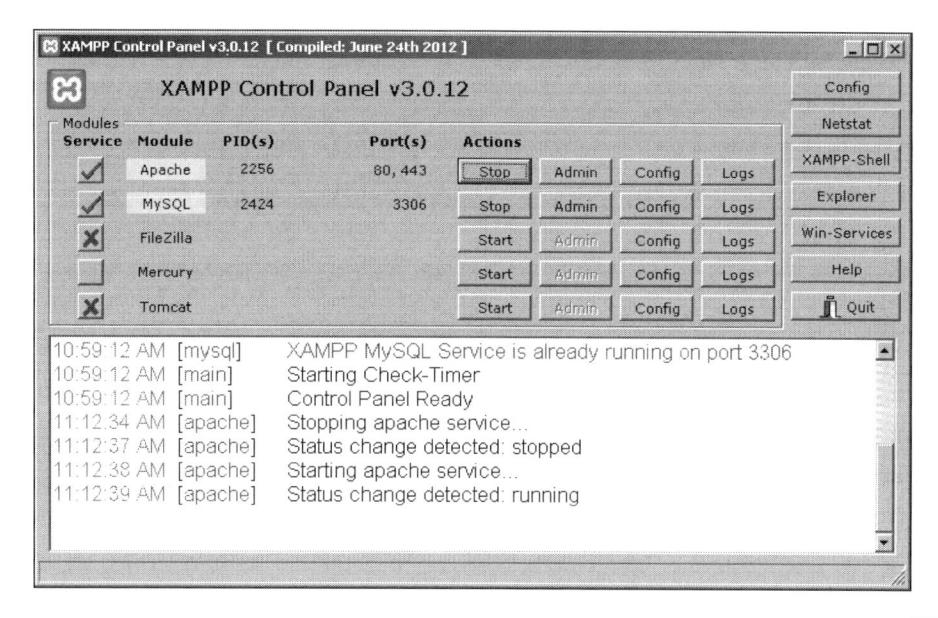

You can see it in the status log area, and the **Stop** button should change its caption to **Start**:

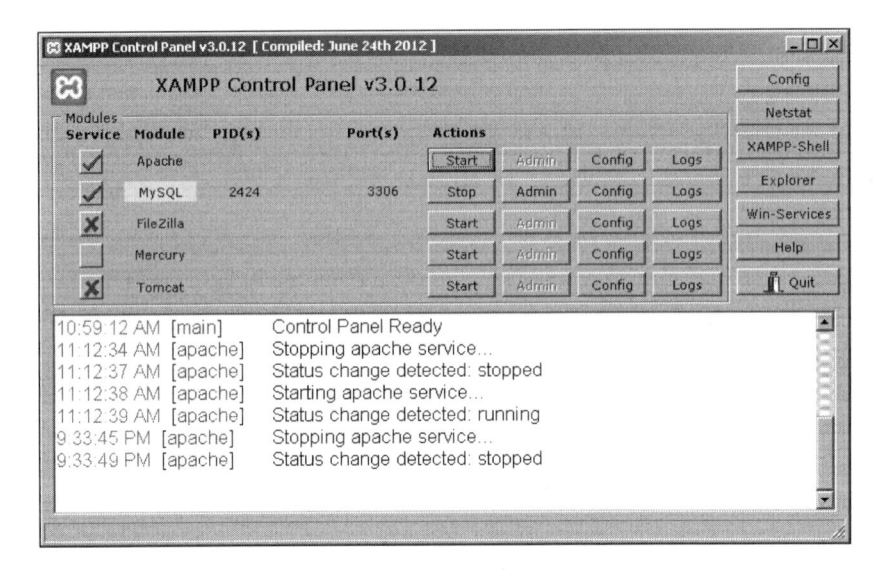

47. Start the Apache server by clicking on the **Start** button.
48. Now, let us check the network access to the Damn Vulnerable Web Application. Start your Windows XP virtual machine if it was stopped and run any web browser.
49. Type `192.168.1.13/dvwa/` into the address bar. You should see the following screenshot:

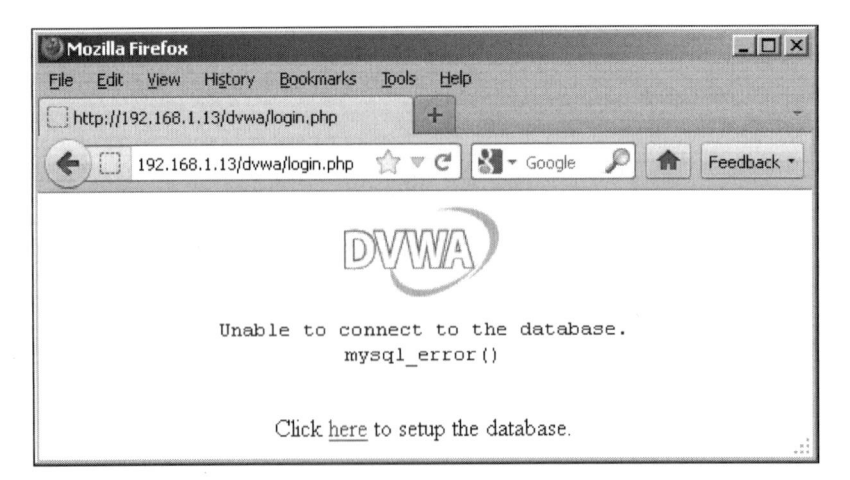

50. The next step is creating a database. Open the link you see in the browser window and you will be redirected to the DVWA control page:

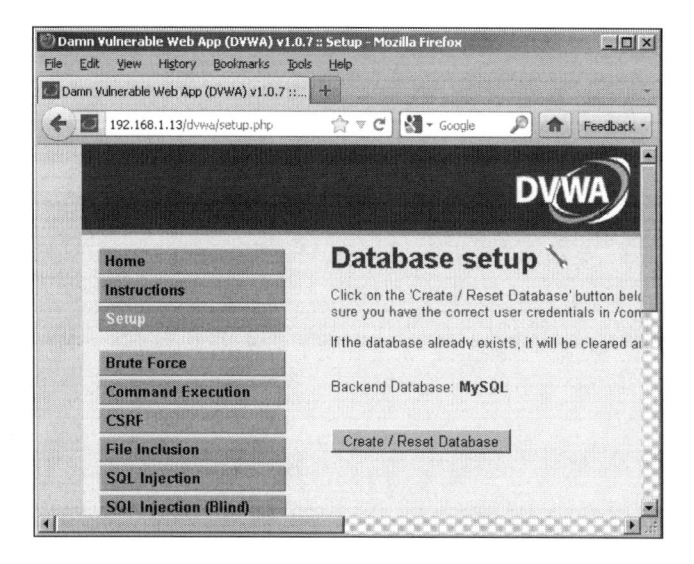

Instant Penetration Testing: Setting Up a Test Lab How-to

51. Click on the **Create / Reset Database** button.
52. In the left-bottom corner of the DVWA control page, you will be able to see that the DVWA security level is set to high:

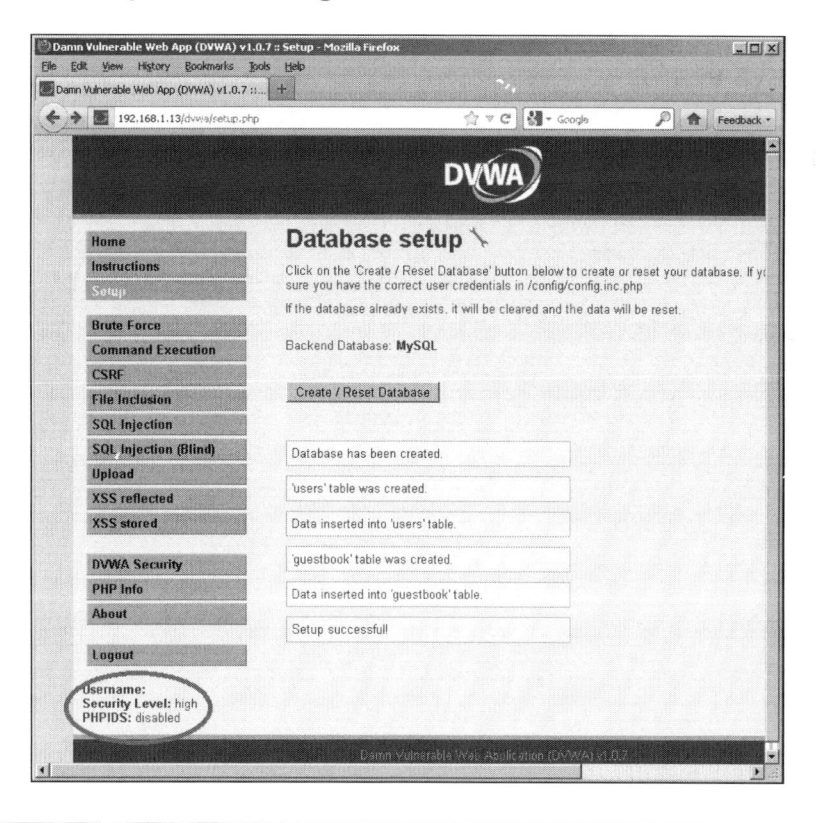

Instant Penetration Testing: Setting Up a Test Lab How-to

53. Let us change it to the low level. Click on the **DVWA Security** button at the left side of the page.

54. In the DVWA login page, type in the username as `admin` and the password as `password`:

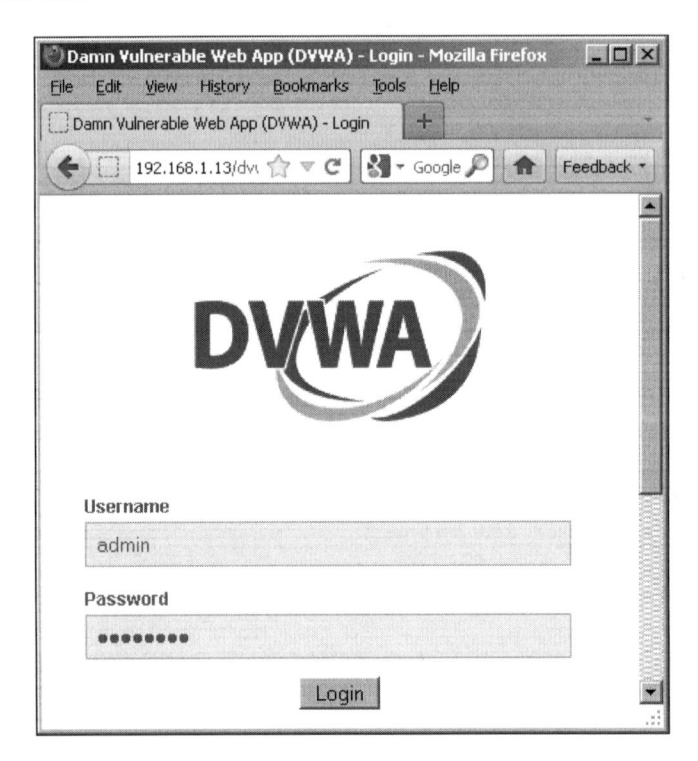

55. Click on the **DVWA Security** button on the left side of the page again.

56. Select the **low** security level in the drop-down menu:

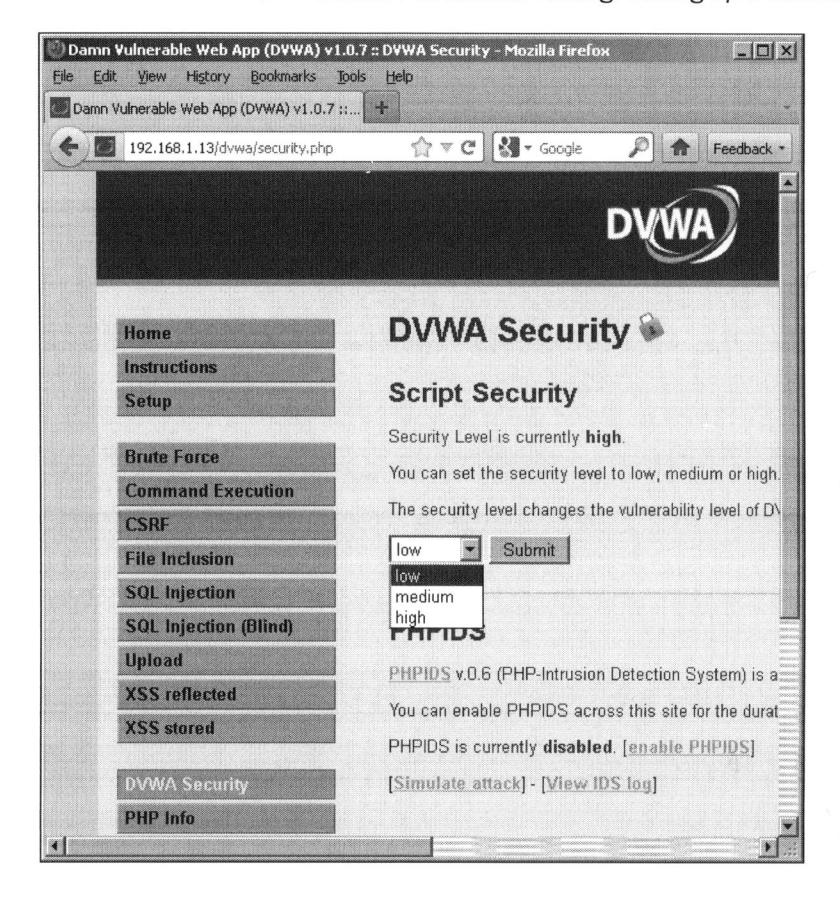

Instant Penetration Testing: Setting Up a Test Lab How-to

57. Then, click on the **Submit** button.
58. Now, take a snapshot; our web server and vulnerable web application are ready for practising web penetration testing skills.

How it works...

Let me explain the essential steps.

At first, we need to configure the router in order to provide our lab with networking capabilities. Then, our virtualization software, which will support the virtual machines, should be installed. After that, we can install and set up our virtual server and workstation.

To truly imitate the real-world scenarios, where different people use various web browsers to access web applications, we need to install several web browsers on our virtual web client machine. I have chosen Google Chrome, Mozilla Firefox, and Apple Safari as victim client browsers, because they are the most popular in real life and you should practice every kind of client-side attack with at least each of these three browsers. Also, I should mention that some kinds of client-side attacks work better with certain browsers and with others, different exploits are aimed at different browsers, and that is why we need several web browsers installed on the victim web client workstation not to restrict our training facilities to only a short list of attack performance.

To leave more opportunities for exploitation, we need to have as many vulnerabilities in web browsers as we can (the more, the better). Fully patched browsers require using the newest exploits, which are hard to find and use because in most cases you will need to personally modify and debug them. So, for successful and productive training, we need to have more older vulnerabilities, and this is the reason why we installed the older versions of web browsers and turned off automatic updates.

The XAMPP package was chosen because it already contains an Apache server, a MySQL server, and PHP configured to work together. It is easy to install, so we don't have to perform any additional configuration to run a web server.

But we need to additionally configure the DVWA access settings to allow access from external clients and not only localhost connections. This is the reason why we edited the `.htaccess` file in a relevant way.

Also we need create a database in DVWA in order to let it work as it should.

For those readers who have already high web penetration testing skills, the high DVWA security level is recommended because they know all the basic techniques and need to practise advanced tricking attack skills. But for beginners I recommend learning basic attack and exploitation techniques with a low DVWA security level to leverage your knowledge step by step.

There's more...

Web application penetration testing is the most rapidly changing security issue and any penetration tester who wants to have up-to-date knowledge needs to constantly learn and train. This section gives you advice on where to look for more information.

Alternative lab options

Let me show you some alternative options of building a web application penetration testing lab.

So, at first, it is not necessary to use a hardware router. Using the built-in VMware Workstation NAT capabilities is enough, but we need a hardware router for other types of labs, so why not use it in this lab as well. Additionally, using a hardware router has a better influence on the lab performance.

Also, you don't have to install the web server on a Windows machine. You can easily use a Linux-based server if you have appropriate knowledge. I should also mention that DVWA is platform independent, so you should not get any troubles installing it on a Linux-based web server.

The web client workstation can be also be a Linux-based system. In addition to this, it is better to have both Windows- and Linux-based client workstations to have a larger field for experimentation.

Alternative vulnerable web app packages

Damn Vulnerable Web Application is not the one and only vulnerable web app that you can use for training in your lab environment.

There are a lot of prepared vulnerable web applications on the Internet that are ready for use with whole virtual server images having vulnerable web app installed. Here is the list of some of them:

- OWASP Broken Web Applications Project (https://www.owasp.org/index.php/OWASP_Broken_Web_Applications_Project)
- NOWASP (Mutillidae) Web Pen-Test Practice Application (http://sourceforge.net/projects/mutillidae/)
- SQLol (https://github.com/SpiderLabs/SQLol)
- Hackxor (http://sourceforge.net/projects/hackxor/)
- Bodgeit (http://code.google.com/p/bodgeit/)

Additional info

Here are some additional information resources:

- http://www.dvwa.co.uk/
- http://www.apachefriends.org/en/xampp.html
- https://www.owasp.org/index.php/Web_Application_Firewall
- https://www.owasp.org/index.php/Category:OWASP_Testing_Project
- https://www.owasp.org/index.php/OWASP_Top_Ten_Project

Instant Penetration Testing: Setting Up a Test Lab How-to

Setting up a Wi-Fi lab (Become an expert)

This section describes how to set up a lab for practising Wi-Fi penetration skills with basic wireless network protection mechanisms.

Skills you can practise using this type of lab are as follows:

- Essential skills
    - Discovery techniques
    - Enumeration techniques
    - Password and hash attacks
    - Wireless attacks
- Additional skills
    - Documenting the penetration testing process

Getting ready

At first, we have to determine the Wi-Fi lab topology and architecture. In this chapter, we will use only those components that are essential for Wi-Fi penetration testing and will not include others. The following lab components are necessary for our current task:

- Wireless router
- LAN workstation
- Victim Wi-Fi client (workstation, laptop, smartphone, or tablet PC)

We will use a direct LAN connection between the LAN workstation and the router, and wireless connections between the victim Wi-Fi client and the wireless router. The topology of that network looks similar to the following diagram:

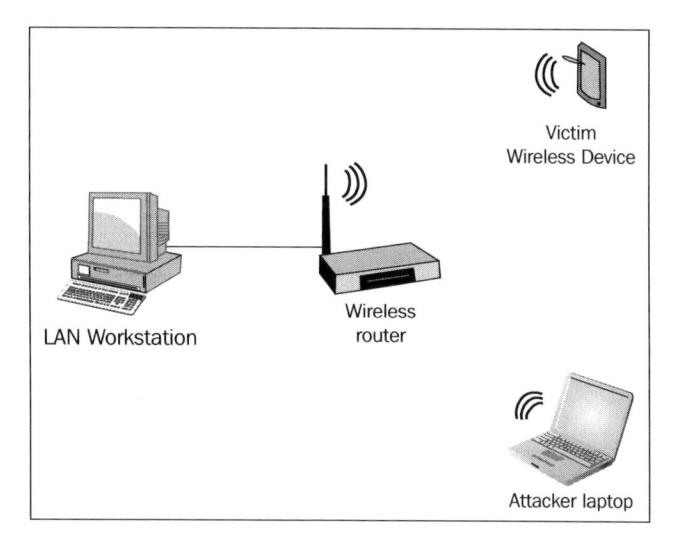

How to do it...

We will set up two Wi-Fi networks of different types. The initial router setup is the same for both types, so I will give the instructions only once before describing the security mechanism's setup. I will use the ASUS WL-520GC router, and all my examples will be given for this model of router.

I want to start by setting up a WEP protected network:

1. Connect your workstation to the router using a LAN cable.
2. Open the browser at the LAN workstation and go to the address `192.168.1.1`.
3. Log in to the router control panel using the default login ID and password `admin:admin` and go to the **Wireless** section.
4. Set the wireless network name (**SSID**) in the corresponding field; for example, set it to `wifilab`.
5. Leave the **Channel** and **Wireless Mode** settings as **Auto**.
6. Set **Authentication Method** as **Shared Key**.
7. Set the **Passphrase** setting value; it will be your key for connecting to the wireless network. Use an easy and not complicated key value, something that can be guessed by a dictionary.
8. Leave all other settings on this page as their default values.

Now, you should have settings similar to the following:

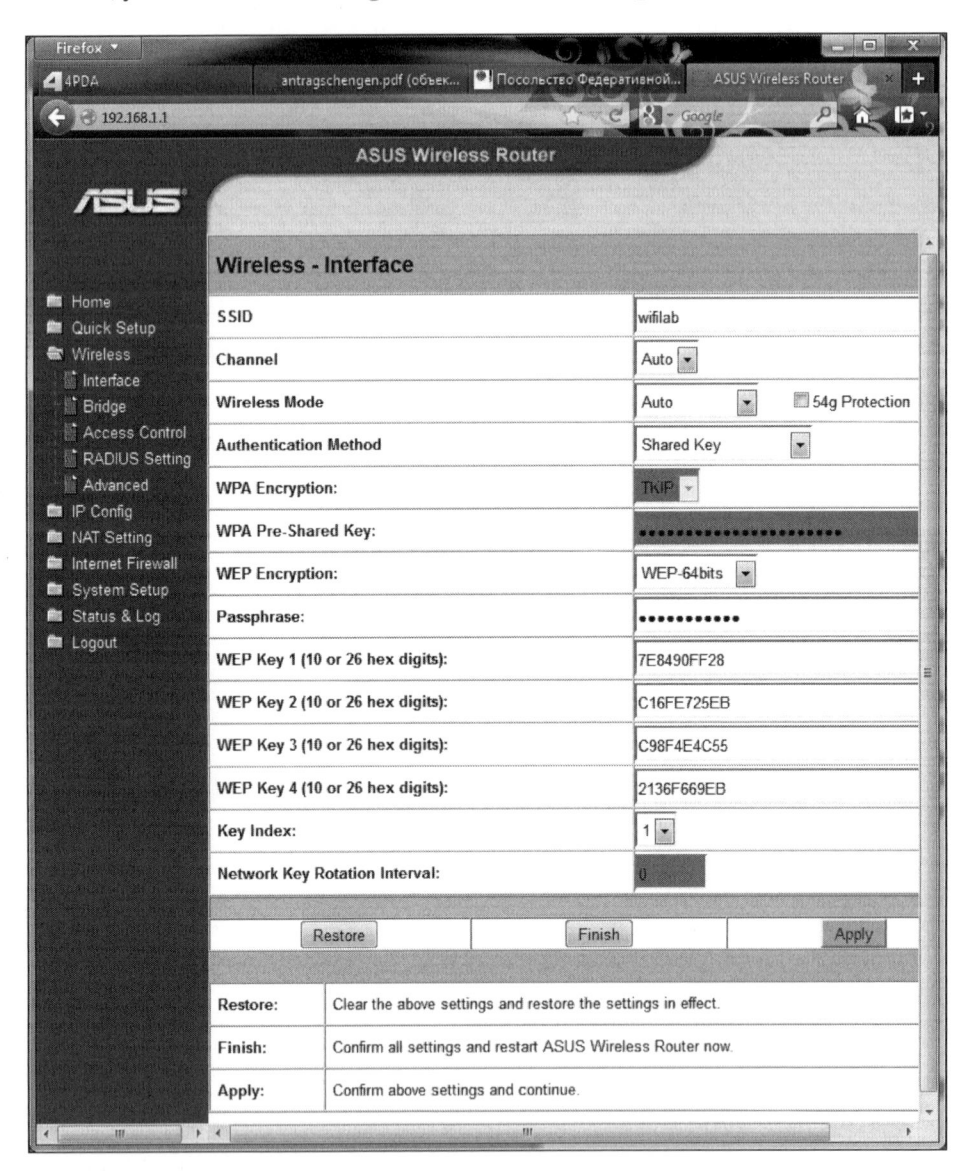

Wireless - Interface

SSID	wifilab
Channel	Auto
Wireless Mode	Auto ☐ 54g Protection
Authentication Method	Shared Key
WPA Encryption:	TKIP
WPA Pre-Shared Key:	••••••••••••••••••••••
WEP Encryption:	WEP-64bits
Passphrase:	••••••••••
WEP Key 1 (10 or 26 hex digits):	7E8490FF28
WEP Key 2 (10 or 26 hex digits):	C16FE725EB
WEP Key 3 (10 or 26 hex digits):	C98F4E4C55
WEP Key 4 (10 or 26 hex digits):	2136F669EB
Key Index:	1
Network Key Rotation Interval:	0

Restore:	Clear the above settings and restore the settings in effect.
Finish:	Confirm all settings and restart ASUS Wireless Router now.
Apply:	Confirm above settings and continue.

9. Now, go to the **Wireless | Advanced** section and set the **Hide SSID** option to **Yes**, leaving all other settings on this page as their default values:

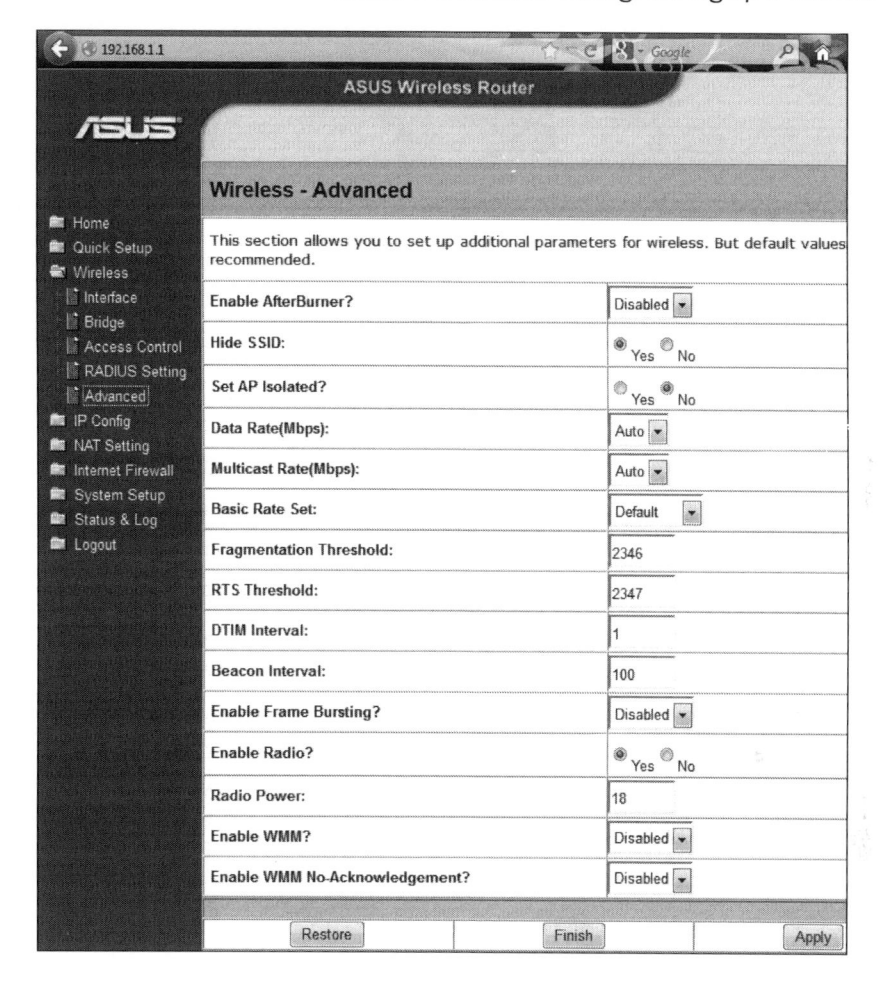

10. Click on **Finish** and then **Save & Restart**.
11. After the router reboots, go to **System setup | Settings Management** and save a backup copy of your current router settings to the file.
12. The WEP protected network is ready for operating now.

After configuring a router, you need to connect your victim Wi-Fi client device to the `wifilab` network. Depending upon the type of your device and its OS, there can be different ways to connect to a wireless network, but the basic steps in general are the same:

1. Enter the wireless network name (**SSID**) – it is `wifilab` in our case.
2. Enter the wireless network passphrase, which you have set during the router configuration process.
3. Click on **Connect**, or **OK**, or whatever button your system offers you to connect to the wireless network.

After setting up a WEP protected wireless network, we can proceed with setting up a more secure WPA-PSK protected network:

1. Log in to the router control panel and go to the **Wireless** section.
2. Set the wireless network name (**SSID**) in the corresponding field; for example, set it to `wifilab` again.
3. Leave the **Channel** and **Wireless Mode** settings as **Auto**.
4. Set **Authentication Method** as **WPA-Personal**.
5. Now, set the value of **WPA Pre-Shared key**. Use something easy and not complicated as a key value, something that can be guessed by a dictionary.
6. You should have settings similar to the following:

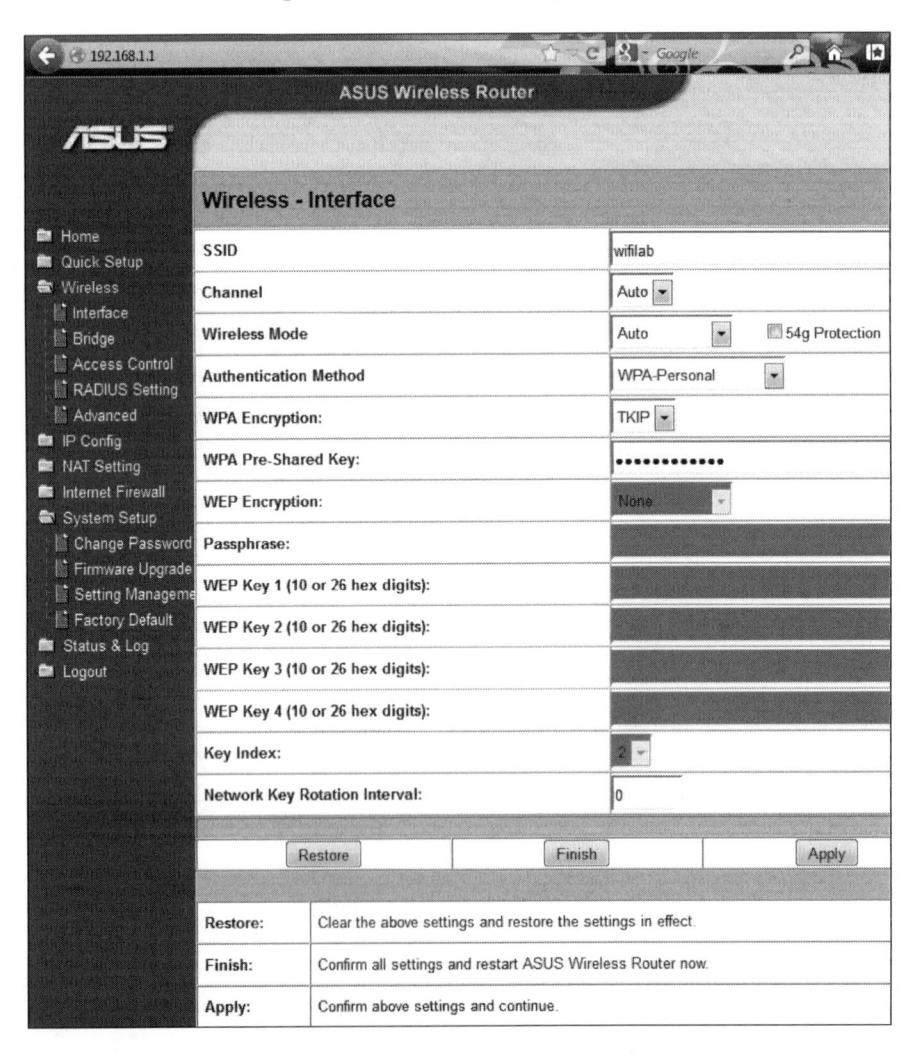

Wireless - Interface	
SSID	wifilab
Channel	Auto
Wireless Mode	Auto — 54g Protection
Authentication Method	WPA-Personal
WPA Encryption:	TKIP
WPA Pre-Shared Key:	....
WEP Encryption:	None
Passphrase:	
WEP Key 1 (10 or 26 hex digits):	
WEP Key 2 (10 or 26 hex digits):	
WEP Key 3 (10 or 26 hex digits):	
WEP Key 4 (10 or 26 hex digits):	
Key Index:	2
Network Key Rotation Interval:	0

Restore:	Clear the above settings and restore the settings in effect.
Finish:	Confirm all settings and restart ASUS Wireless Router now.
Apply:	Confirm above settings and continue.

7. Now, go to **Wireless | Advanced**, and set the **Hide SSID** option to **Yes**, leaving all other settings on this page as their default values:

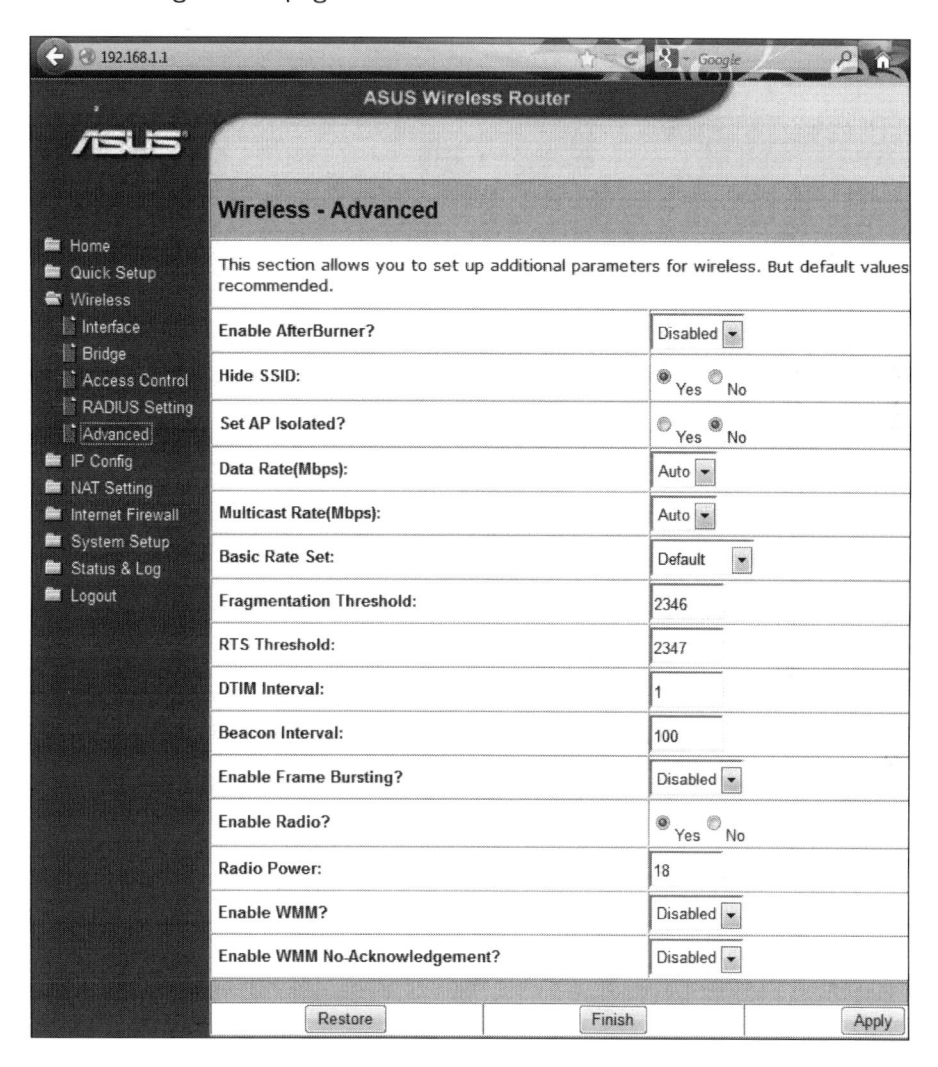

8. Click on **Finish** and then **Save & Restart**.
9. After the router reboots, go to the **System setup | Settings Management**, and save a backup copy of your current router settings to the file.
10. The WPA-PSK protected network is ready for operating now.

Now, you need to connect your victim Wi-Fi client device to the `wifilab` network in the same way as it was described in the *Planning the lab environment (Should know)* recipe.

How it works...

I would like to give you some explanation of the described steps in this section.

I have chosen the network topology based on real-world penetration testing scenarios. We need at least one wireless client connected to the wireless network, because most of the attacks require both a communicating wireless access point and a client. We also need a LAN workstation in order to practise penetration in the LAN through WLAN.

I recommend using simple and easy guessing values for the WEP and WPA password phrases to facilitate password guessing, which you will perform while practising wireless attacks.

I also recommend saving your router configuration backups in order to easily revert the router to the needed state without having to repeat all the configuration steps every time.

It is necessary to restart the router every time after changing its configuration in order to apply new settings.

There's more...

As usual, if you do not want to limit yourself to only the given steps, then there is more information in the following sections to help you choose your next steps.

Improving your hacker skills

An advanced hacker has to be an expert in every type of security, including Wi-Fi WPA-Enterprise protection. So, if you want to become a highly qualified Wi-Fi penetration testing expert, I recommend you to additionally set up a Radius server in your lab network and connect the router to it for practising WPA-Enterprise protection hacking.

It is better done with a virtual Linux machine and free-radius software. You will need to install a virtual Linux host with a bridged network interface configured to use a static IP address. The network topology with the Radius server will look similar to the following diagram:

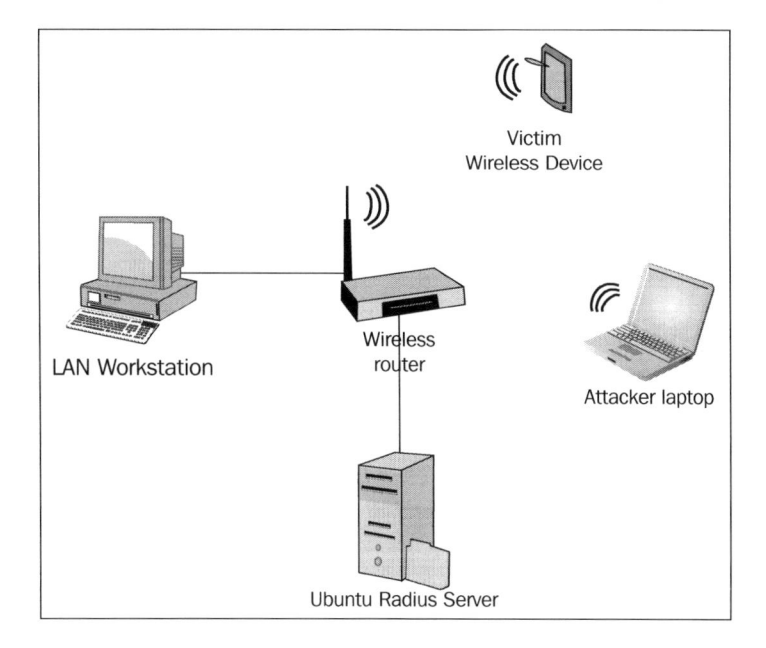

Instant Penetration Testing: Setting Up a Test Lab How-to

After creating a virtual Linux machine, you will need to install the free-radius software. The easiest way to do it is to use `apt-get` command:

```
sudo apt-get install -yu free-radius
```

Or:

```
sudo apt-get install -yu free-radius-wpe
```

`free-radius-wpe` is the modified version of `free-radius` and is mostly used for hacking purposes, but you can also use it just for creating a Radius server.

After installing, you will need to edit some configuration files in order to set the connection key, which will be used by the router to work with a Radius server, and set up account settings to let users connect to the wireless network via WPA-Enterprise.

At the end, you need to set the Radius server IP address, port number, and connection key in the router settings. Reboot the router.

Tips

Most Wi-Fi routers support the WPS protocol (Wi-Fi Protected setup: `http://www.wi-fi.org/knowledge-center/articles/wi-fi-protected-setup%E2%84%A2`), which allows us to easily connect devices to the wireless network. But recently, WPS was compromised and is now considered unsafe. Also, the WPS key can be guessed in less than 30 hours.

You can learn how to do it at `http://www.ehacking.net/2012/01/reaver-wps-wpawpa2-cracking-tutorial.html`.

It is often necessary to guess the WPA keys by using a dictionary, but such procedures take a lot of time with big dictionaries. That is why I recommend using cloud services to easily and quickly test hashes with big dictionaries. For example, I use this service: `http://www.cloudcracker.com`.

Another thing worth mentioning is the wireless interface with packet injection capabilities on the attacker's machine, which is essential for successful wireless attacks. It could be Wi-Fi cards based on Atheros or Prism chipsets. For example, I use the ALFA Network AWUS036NH wireless USB adapter.

Additional info

I recommend that you check the following books to improve your Wi-Fi penetration testing skills to an advanced level:

- *Johnny Cache, Vincent Liu. Hacking Wireless Exposed: Wireless Security Secrets & Solutions*, Second Edition
- *Andrew Vladimirov, Konstantin V. Gavrilenko, Andrei A. Mikhailovsky. Wi-Foo: The Secrets of Wireless Hacking*
- *Rob Flickenger, Roger Weeks. Wireless Hacks: Tips & Tools for Building, Extending, and Securing Your Network*, Second Edition

If you are going to become a Wi-Fi penetration testing expert, you should definitely check the following web resources:

- Aircrack-Ng wireless attack toolset: `http://www.aircrack-ng.org/`
- Wireless penetration testing methodology: `http://wirelessdefence.org/Contents/Wireless%20Pen%20Test%20Framework.html`

Instant Penetration Testing: Setting Up a Test Lab How-to

Reviewing online lab portals (Become an expert)

In this section, I will make short reviews of public online penetration testing labs on the Internet, which are being held by third parties.

Getting ready

Nowadays, there are a lot of such online penetration testing lab portals available, which offer plenty of various network services and lab environment topologies suitable for almost any training tasks and needs. But, there is at least one common thing with them that is important for any junior penetration tester – you do not need to install, set up, and maintain any hardware or software on your own; it is already done for you.

It is worth mentioning that you cannot change all lab components settings and this is the reason why they are not suitable for some kinds of specific tasks, which demand configuring specific lab environment parameters.

To start training with online penetration testing labs, you will need the following:

- A computer with Internet access
- A web browser
- An e-mail address, which will be used only for working with online penetration testing lab portals and will not be connected to your other e-mail accounts
- BackTrack 5R3 virtual machine

How to do it...

Let us check some online lab portals with a short description of each. We will start by examining "Hacking-Lab" – one of the most interesting online hacking portals, which offers you various online hacking challenges, including OWASP TOP 10 trainings:

Instant Penetration Testing: Setting Up a Test Lab How-to

1. Open your browser and enter the address as `https://www.hacking-lab.com/`. You should see the following page:

2. Click on **Remote Security Lab** on the left side of the main page, then click on **Topology** to see that the **Hacking Lab** portal consists of two logical parts: **Public web portal** and **VPN-protected lab network**:

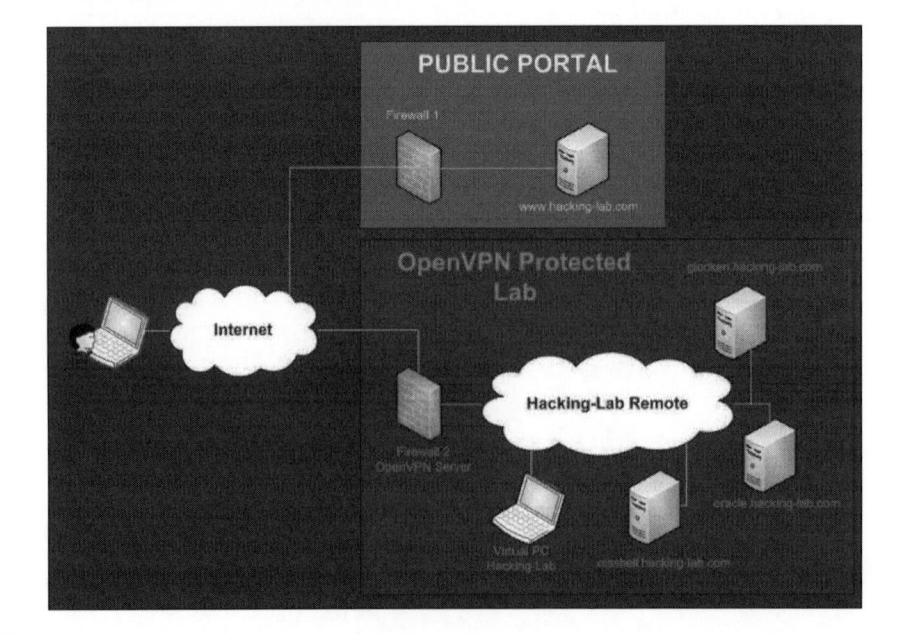

To start using the Hacking Lab programs, you need to register and log in with your account.

3. Click on **Create a free account now!** on the left side of the web page and register.

4. Click on the **Events** link to check which events are available at the moment:

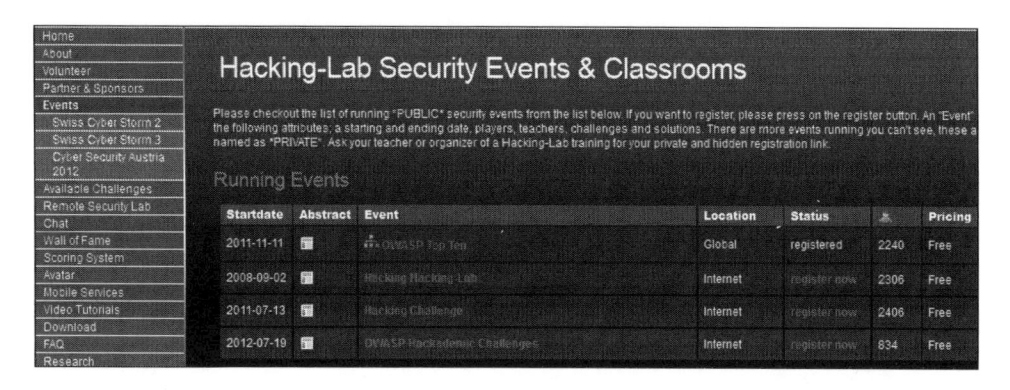

5. Choose the event and click on **Register Now** in the **Status** column. In my case, it is **OWASP Top Ten**.

6. Return to the **Events** page, click on the event that you have chosen and select the challenge from the opened list to read details.

Some of the events require a VPN connection to the lab. Let me show you how to establish it with **OWASP Top Ten event #1 - OWASP A1 - Blind SQL Injection Attack**. Remember that you will be allowed to establish a connection only if you are registered to one of the events which requires it.

1. Click on the **Download** link on the left side of the web page and choose **LiveCD**.

2. Select the last version and download **VMware8 Appliance**.

3. Now, run VMware Workstation and select **Open** in the **File** menu and select the **LiveCD VMware8 Appliance** in the new dialog window.

4. In the **Import Virtual Machine** dialog window, set the virtual machine name directory and click on **Import**.

5. Run the LiveCD virtual machine:

6. Click on the flag icon at the top-right corner and change the keyboard layout to **US**.
7. Now, right-click on the VPN connection icon next to keyboard layout and select **Connect Password**. The following window will be opened:

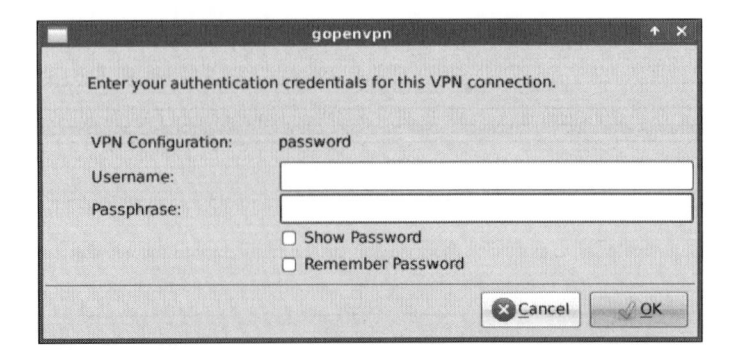

8. Enter your Hacking-Lab ID (e-mail) with the initial password and click on **OK**. The VPN connection icon at the top-right corner should become green if everything was correct.

9. Now, open the browser and enter the vulnerable application URL: `http://glocken.hacking-lab.com/12001/inputval_case2/inputval2/index.html`.

10. Start solving the challenge!

Now, let us take a look at another portal called Hack-a-Server.

This portal is used not only by white-hat hackers and penetration testers who want to improve their skills, but also by system administrators and owners of real servers who want to test its security and are ready to pay for vulnerabilities disclosure. You can find the main idea of that portal right at its home page.

Instant Penetration Testing: Setting Up a Test Lab How-to

1. Open the browser and enter the address as `https://www.hackaserver.com/`.

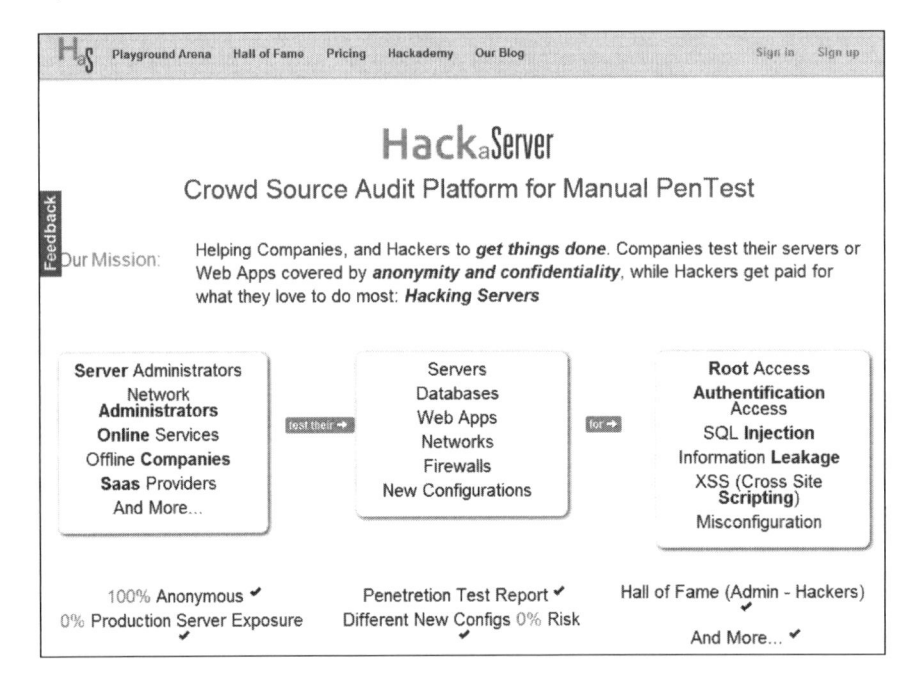

2. Click on **Sign Up** at the top right-corner of the page.
3. Enter your nickname, e-mail, password, and click on **Sign Up**.
4. Check your e-mail; you will receive a message from the Hack-A-Server portal containing your account activation link. Click on the link.

Only Training and Exam arenas are available for you in this step. But, it is worth mentioning that Hack-A-Server is a commercial start up and that is why it allows you to earn money for vulnerabilities disclosure and exploitation at the playground arena.

But, before you can access the playground arena where money could be earned, you have to pass the exam.

1. Click on the **Training Arena** link at the top of the web page and check what is available for practising your penetration testing skills:

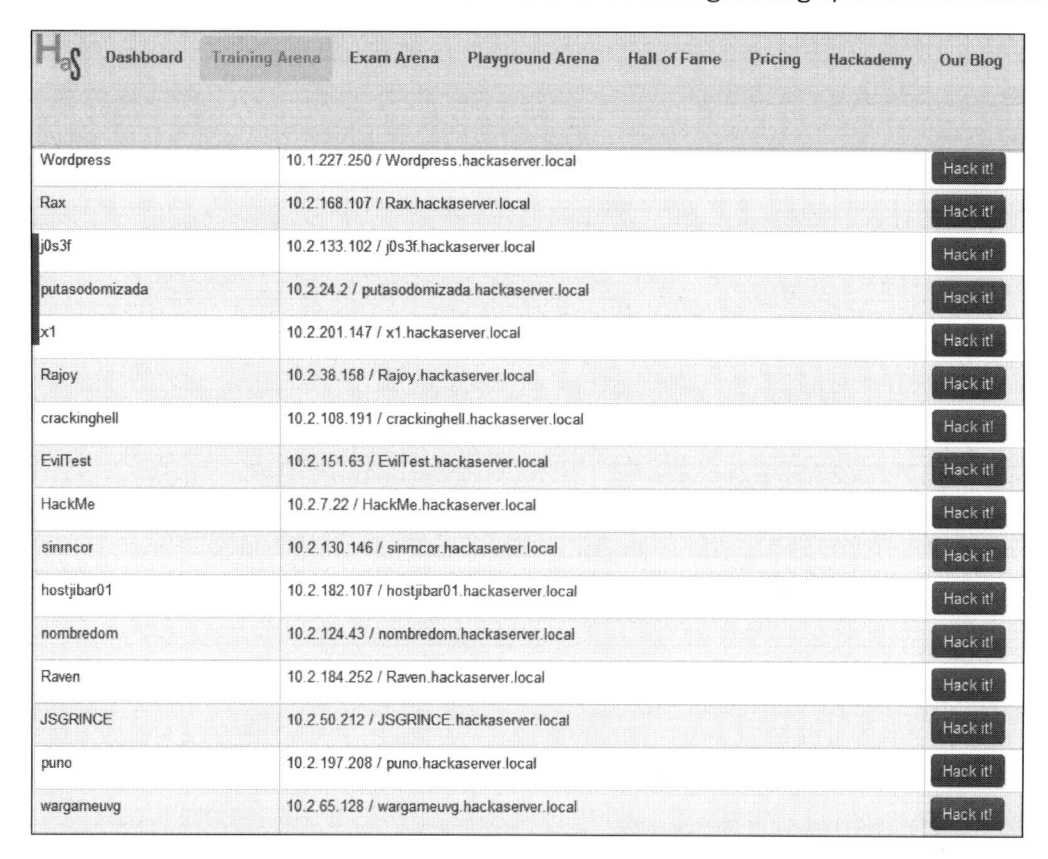

Wordpress	10.1.227.250 / Wordpress.hackaserver.local	Hack it!
Rax	10.2.168.107 / Rax.hackaserver.local	Hack it!
j0s3f	10.2.133.102 / j0s3f.hackaserver.local	Hack it!
putasodomizada	10.2.24.2 / putasodomizada.hackaserver.local	Hack it!
x1	10.2.201.147 / x1.hackaserver.local	Hack it!
Rajoy	10.2.38.158 / Rajoy.hackaserver.local	Hack it!
crackinghell	10.2.108.191 / crackinghell.hackaserver.local	Hack it!
EvilTest	10.2.151.63 / EvilTest.hackaserver.local	Hack it!
HackMe	10.2.7.22 / HackMe.hackaserver.local	Hack it!
sinmcor	10.2.130.146 / sinmcor.hackaserver.local	Hack it!
hostjibar01	10.2.182.107 / hostjibar01.hackaserver.local	Hack it!
nombredom	10.2.124.43 / nombredom.hackaserver.local	Hack it!
Raven	10.2.184.252 / Raven.hackaserver.local	Hack it!
JSGRINCE	10.2.50.212 / JSGRINCE.hackaserver.local	Hack it!
puno	10.2.197.208 / puno.hackaserver.local	Hack it!
wargameuvg	10.2.65.128 / wargameuvg.hackaserver.local	Hack it!

2. Select any target and click on **Hack It!** to view the target details.
3. The portal will ask you to download the certificate bundle (connection package) to create a VPN connection to the training arena.
4. Download the certificate bundle and unzip it.
5. Start the BackTrack 5R3 virtual machine.
6. Copy the unzipped connection package to your virtual BackTrack 5R3 machine.
7. Open the terminal and change the working directory to the certificate bundle directory.

8. Run the following command:

   ```
   openvpn client.conf
   ```

9. Now, open a new terminal window and check the connection to the target by trace routing and pinging its IP address (you can find it on the target details web page):

   ```
   root@bt:~# traceroute 10.2.7.22
   traceroute to 10.2.7.22 (10.2.7.22), 30 hops max, 60 byte packets
    1  10.8.0.1 (10.8.0.1)  55.114 ms  55.143 ms  55.146 ms
    2  10.2.7.22 (10.2.7.22)  59.159 ms  59.179 ms  59.211 ms
   root@bt:~# ping 10.2.7.22
   PING 10.2.7.22 (10.2.7.22) 56(84) bytes of data.
   64 bytes from 10.2.7.22: icmp_seq=1 ttl=63 time=55.5 ms
   64 bytes from 10.2.7.22: icmp_seq=2 ttl=63 time=55.3 ms
   64 bytes from 10.2.7.22: icmp_seq=3 ttl=63 time=55.1 ms
   ^C
   --- 10.2.7.22 ping statistics ---
   3 packets transmitted, 3 received, 0% packet loss, time 2003ms
   rtt min/avg/max/mdev = 55.131/55.363/55.588/0.329 ms
   root@bt:~#
   ```

10. Now hack it!

To pass the exam, you will have to find as many vulnerabilities as you can at the exam arena and submit a report to the Hack-a-Server team for review. If you pass the exam, you will be allowed into the playground arena, where you can get paid for hacking.

There's more...

If you are interested in trying as many online hacking playgrounds as possible, you should definitely check the following ones too:

- `http://try2hack.nl`
- `http://www.hackthissite.org`
- `http://www.dareyourmind.net`
- `http://www.hackquest.com/`
- `http://www.root-me.org`
- `http://hax.tor.hu`

[PACKT PUBLISHING] Thank you for buying Penetration Testing: Setting up a test lab How-To

About Packt Publishing

Packt, pronounced 'packed', published its first book "*Mastering phpMyAdmin for Effective MySQL Management*" in April 2004 and subsequently continued to specialize in publishing highly focused books on specific technologies and solutions.

Our books and publications share the experiences of your fellow IT professionals in adapting and customizing today's systems, applications, and frameworks. Our solution based books give you the knowledge and power to customize the software and technologies you're using to get the job done. Packt books are more specific and less general than the IT books you have seen in the past. Our unique business model allows us to bring you more focused information, giving you more of what you need to know, and less of what you don't.

Packt is a modern, yet unique publishing company, which focuses on producing quality, cutting-edge books for communities of developers, administrators, and newbies alike. For more information, please visit our website: `www.packtpub.com`.

Writing for Packt

We welcome all inquiries from people who are interested in authoring. Book proposals should be sent to `author@packtpub.com`. If your book idea is still at an early stage and you would like to discuss it first before writing a formal book proposal, contact us; one of our commissioning editors will get in touch with you.

We're not just looking for published authors; if you have strong technical skills but no writing experience, our experienced editors can help you develop a writing career, or simply get some additional reward for your expertise.

Metasploit Penetration Testing Cookbook

ISBN: 978-1-849517-42-3   Paperback: 268 pages

Over 70 recipes to master the most widely used penetration testing framework

1. More than 80 recipes/practicaltasks that will escalate the reader's knowledge from beginner to an advanced level

2. Special focus on the latest operating systems, exploits, and penetration testing techniques

3. Detailed analysis of third party tools based on the Metasploit framework to enhance the penetration testing experience

Advanced Penetration Testing for Highly-Secured Environments: The Ultimate Security Guide

ISBN: 978-1-849517-74-4   Paperback: 414 pages

Learn to perform proffessional penetration testing for highly-secured environments with the intensive hands-on guide

1. Learn how to perform an efficient, organized, and effective penetration test from start to finish

2. Gain hands-on penetration testing experience by building and testing a virtual lab environment that includes commonly found security measures such as IDS and firewalls

3. Take the challenge and perform a virtual penetration test against a fictional corporation from start to finish and then verify your results by walking through step-by-step solutions

Please check **www.PacktPub.com** for information on our titles

[PACKT] PUBLISHING

BackTrack 4: Assuring Security by Penetration Testing

ISBN: 978-1-849513-94-4   Paperback: 392 pages

Master the art of penetration testing with BackTrack

1. Learn the black-art of penetration testing with in-depth coverage of BackTrack Linux distribution
2. Explore the insights and importance of testing your corporate network systems before hackers strike it
3. Understand the practical spectrum of security tools by their exemplary usage, configuration, and benefits

BackTrack 5 Wireless Penetration Testing Beginner's Guide

ISBN: 978-1-849515-58-0   Paperback: 220 pages

Master bleeding edge wireless testing techniques with BackTrack 5

1. Learn Wireless Penetration Testing with the most recent version of Backtrack
2. The first and only book that covers wireless testing with BackTrack
3. Concepts explained with step-by-step practical sessions and rich illustrations
4. Written by Vivek Ramachandran – world renowned security research and evangelist, and discoverer of the wireless "Caffe Latte Attack"

Please check www.PacktPub.com for information on our titles

Printed in Great Britain
by Amazon.co.uk, Ltd.,
Marston Gate.